616.6

D0398131

unmedicated.

Center Point
Large Print

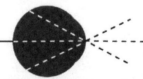

**This Large Print Book carries the
Seal of Approval of N.A.V.H.**

unmedicated.

THE FOUR PILLARS
OF NATURAL WELLNESS

MADISYN TAYLOR

CENTER POINT LARGE PRINT
THORNDIKE, MAINE

Library of Congress Cataloging-in-Publication Data

Names: Taylor, Madisyn.
Title: Unmedicated : the four pillars of natural wellness / Madisyn Taylor.
Description: Large print edition. | Thorndike, Maine :
    Center Point Large Print, 2018.
Identifiers: LCCN 2018003805 | ISBN 9781683247760
    (hardcover : alk. paper)
Subjects: LCSH: Mind and body therapies—Methodology. |
    Depression, Mental—Alternative treatment. | Anxiety disorders—
    Alternative treatment. | Large type books.
Classification: LCC RC489.M53 T39 2018a | DDC 616.6/1—dc23
LC record available at https://lccn.loc.gov/2018003805

Contents

Foreword

We are now at a tipping point in our approach to psychological and psychiatric issues. The drug approach—that there is a pill for every ailment—has not lived up to its promise. The 1990s decade was all about the brain, and many incredible discoveries in neuroscience have been made since in our understanding of how the brain functions. These discoveries have also shown us how incredibly complex the brain is and how much more we have to learn.

The brain is an organ that is subject to all the genetic and environmental insults it accrues over the years. Inflammation, toxicity, head trauma, vascular insufficiency, and endocrine issues all affect our mind, mood, and behavior. We need to lower our toxic burden of heavy metals, chemicals, and pesticides. We need to lower inflammation in our brains through proper diet and adequate antioxidants. Special care should be given to avoid head trauma in our children and young adults. We also need to supply our brains with the proper vitamins, minerals, amino acids, and hormones so the brain has what it needs to function properly. Most important, we need to deal with the stress in our lives.

Stress plays a crucial part in brain health. Most patients I see are extremely stressed. When we are stressed, in that fight-or-flight mode, we are destroying brain cells by the millions. In *Unmedicated*, Madisyn shows how to take responsibility for your mental health, how to lower your stress levels, how to preserve your brain function, and how to be happier in your life.

We all need to take responsibility for our situations. So often, we go to a health practitioner looking for the magic pill to make us better. Medication can be helpful at times, but it is only part of the solution. Usually, our symptoms are only the tip of the iceberg. Discovering the why rather than just the name of what we are experiencing leads to self-discovery and a more lasting cure. An analogy I use is a ceiling with ten holes in it. A medication may be effective in plugging up one or two of the holes, but that still leaves eight holes open. The track record of psychiatric medication has fallen short. The result is often only slightly better than a placebo but with intolerable side effects. This is why when medication must be used, it should be in a holistic, functional-medicine setting.

Clear your mind, nurture your spirit, strengthen your body, and find your tribe. These four pillars of natural wellness taught in this book are all worthy goals to work toward. A clear mind allows you to see reality the way it is and to make the necessary changes in your life. When your mind is activated by emotional stress, neuroscience has shown that you don't see reality clearly and often make unhealthy or improper choices. When your spirit is nurtured, you feel connected to something bigger and more powerful than yourself. You become curious, open, less defensive, and integrated. As your body strengthens, it allows your mind to become more clear, and you can enjoy the energy and vitality you deserve. Health is a function of participation: the more you isolate yourself, the sicker you will become. Finding your tribe—your community— allows you to participate and be supported by like-minded people.

I am grateful and honored that Madisyn asked me to write a foreword for this timely and important book. This is a book to be with; to study; to stand in, with its questions; and to let penetrate your soul.

David R. Allen, MD

Introduction

It is my heartfelt intention to share with you how I healed my unhealthy reliance on medication. In sharing my own experience of healing, it is my wish to help you on your own path to wellness.

You will learn of my roller-coaster ride with antidepressants and antianxiety medications, and my journey through many tests and doctors. You will see that I finally landed on a very different shore—a place of health using natural, holistic methods available to everybody—because I knew I didn't want to spend my life medicated and ill.

It is important to know that I am not against medication; I believe strongly in the myriad benefits of medicine and the medical community. I am grateful for all their work. What I am offering in this book is information and alternative choices.

Before I share the good news, though, I feel it's important to also share with you the story of how I came to the place of being so unwell, how my journey over fifty years of experience and practice led me to a life of wholeness and balance, and how I created a step-by-step program that allows me to live my life free and unmedicated. Often, it is through the personal experience of others that we learn the most and receive the inspiration necessary to begin our own healing journey.

My Story:
From Medicated to Unmedicated

My depression and anxiety manifested because of unresolved mental-health issues. I lived with depression and anxiety for so long that I didn't know it was a medical problem. It was simply how I always was; it was all I ever knew.

Because I was born highly sensitive (a deep sense of feeling emotions and highly attuned to stimuli), the emotional abuse and resultant traumas I experienced in my household growing up changed my wiring, my chemistry. I adapted for survival and never dealt with the hurt and painful feelings I experienced as a child and young adult. I had no idea this would come back to haunt me later in life, but why would I? When you're in survival mode, that's what takes priority in your life—surviving.

When I look back at my childhood, I see so many early signs that I was in trouble and particularly vulnerable to being unwell. My body tended to react to mental distress with physical illness in one form or another. My first panic attack happened around third grade. To this day, I remember lying in bed at night, thinking about death and what happens when you die. As I lay there thinking that I would never exist again for billions of years, the thought overwhelmed me, and I bolted upright in my bed, gasping for breath. The dreadful fear was unbearable, yet I could not turn to my parents; they never talked about these kinds of important issues. I could not depend on them for comfort.

My father was intimidating and prone to outbursts of rage, so as a little girl, I realized quickly that it was best to keep quiet and remain invisible in the household rather than do anything to trigger his fury. I now believe he probably suffered from an undiagnosed chemical imbalance, as there were periods of time when he was nice and even happy. It became natural for me to sense his energy, but even when I thought it was a safe day, I was always on high alert to avoid unleashing one of his terrifying explosions. My mother, brother, and I lived with a constant dread. "Every man for himself" quickly became normal in our household. Imagine how difficult it was for an already sensitive girl to not even be able to go to her own mother for the protection and support she needed. With every incident, I shut down more and more. With every incident, I developed more survival skills. Now, when I look back at myself as a young girl, I weep for that child. At the time, I had no choice but to carry on knowing that someday, I would leave that house and my life would be mine to live.

I spent a lot of time in my bedroom alone, with the door locked, and I even went so far as to make a special safe place in the closet by hanging pictures and bringing in a lamp and pillows. When my father went into one of his rampages, I retreated into my closet and held my hands over my ears, crying and rocking back and forth to comfort myself.

Sadly, my father never told me he loved me until I was an adult, and that was after I initiated the conversation. As a child, I believe the only time I felt any feelings of warmth from him was when I was sick, as I knew he would not yell at me then. My mother told me that when I was a toddler, I always wanted to put on a dress before Daddy came home from work—I was already trying to win his approval. Nothing was ever good enough for him, though; he was always lecturing me on how to behave in public, how to behave at friends' houses, how to talk to adults, how the house should look, how I should look. Sometime in high school, I think he gave up on me, deciding I would never amount to anything; he called me a "flunky," although I had never actually flunked anything. These incidents happened with every report card or test result. I never lived up to his perfect expectations of who I should be. I knew that even if I received straight As, it would not be good enough; there would always be something to point out that I was doing wrong.

Other drama that manifested as trauma to me happened in my life outside of my father's verbally and emotionally abusive actions. I can recall specific times in my life when major shifts had a huge impact on me. The last day of elementary school was one of those days. It happened to be my birthday, and the entire school was sitting outside, receiving our sendoff from the principal. Even as a sixth grader, I experienced the deep insight that my life wouldn't be the same again. A place I had known and enjoyed for seven years would disappear from my life: a place where I had excelled in school and was popular, where a lot of other kids liked me. I'm not sure if I was having a psychic moment of foresight or not, but it was incredibly real for me, this knowing that nothing would ever be the same.

Indeed it wasn't, for on the first day of junior high school, I experienced tremendous fear and isolation. Being forced into a very large school with older kids scared me. I was a small, shy, and naïve girl thrust into a school with kids from the opposite side of the tracks that I had very little in common with. The junior high was so big that I rarely had friends I knew in class, even those I had been friends with in elementary school.

The kids were funneled into this big school from all around town, which meant some came from crime-ridden neighborhoods. It wasn't long before a fight broke out in the hallway, and I would have leapt out of my body in that moment if I could have. School had always been safe for me compared to what I was experiencing at home. Elementary school had been a haven. Now I was on high alert at the place where I was supposed to receive my education. And like I had when I felt insecure at home, I learned to keep my head down and mind my own business, which made it difficult for me to build a support system of peers. If I saw some rough kids, I walked the other way; and when fighting broke out, I made a mad dash for my classroom.

It was during this time that I became aware of changes that didn't agree with me: bigger schools, bigger hallways, bigger classes, more noise, and harsh lighting. Nobody knew in those days how acute and overwhelming outside stimulation can be to a highly sensitive person—and even if they had, I'm sure nothing would have been done or explained to me. Due to the large size of the school, the teachers didn't take notice of me. Bigger problems, like dealing with the delinquent kids, took priority. I dug deeper into survival mode, trying to get through each day until I could hide in my bed and make it all go away.

When it was time to go to high school for ninth grade, my parents decided to send me to a private Catholic school even though we weren't Catholic. This upheaval—both the transition to high school and the shift to a stricter, more demanding teaching style within a rigorous religion I didn't practice—brought additional unsettling changes. Plus, there was the added wrench of teenagers going through puberty and surging hormones. Not me—I was a late bloomer and the boys made sure to let me know.

Because it was a private school, there was no fighting in the halls, and this was a tremendous relief to me. By this point, however, my anxiety and extreme shyness were in full swing. I didn't know very many kids at this school—just a handful out of a class of 365 kids.

Most people either love high school or hate it, and I was of the latter group. As I progressed through the grades and my own hormones kicked in, suicidal thoughts started coming more frequently. I turned to experimentation with drugs, alcohol, and boys to silence those thoughts, hide my suffering, and find what I thought was love. Engaging in these activities made me feel powerful and in control—feelings nobody could take away from me.

It was during this time of my life that I experienced another blow to my feelings of safety: events that would forever shape me as a person and have one of the biggest impacts on my life. When I was fifteen years old, I was having a typical night at home—my father yelling at somebody and me wanting to escape—and I just couldn't take it anymore. I didn't have a driver's license or a car, but I needed to get out or go crazy. So I ran out of my house.

I walked about a mile as the sun was beginning to set, realizing I should head home—no good would come from being out in the dark alone. A man was walking toward me, and it gave me a weird feeling—something was not right. My survival and intuitive instincts were fully engaged. I crossed the road so I wouldn't have to meet him. I was walking quickly away, but I turned around and saw that he was now following me. *Oh God, what am I going to do? What is going to happen to me?* Before I could think about what to do next, he came up from behind and grabbed me with both of his hands around my waist. He began to throw me toward a ditch and some bushes.

What happened next was a bit of a blur, as about a million thoughts occurred in a few seconds. Have you ever had a dream where the boogieman is going to get you and you try to scream but nothing comes out? I couldn't let that happen! I opened my mouth and made a sound I didn't know was possible. The sound of survival came from the very depth of my being—a primal, raw scream so loud it shocked me. I screamed my survival scream until he let go and ran off with the comment, "Scared you!"

By now it was fairly dark, and I was a kid alone who had just been attacked. The survivor in me knew to walk two blocks more to a pay phone and call home. My brother came and picked me up, and I didn't talk about it again until now. Because I was afraid of getting into trouble, I didn't tell my parents. It was my fault I was out at night alone, walking far from home—my mistake. No, it was best to stuff down that experience and all the accompanying emotions—terror, shock, panic—and just try to get through another day as I had done with other trauma-tizing experiences. Sadly, I thought this was what life was like: the world was a cruel and unsafe place.

While the chances of this happening to some-body are pretty rare, the chance that it could happen twice seems almost impossible. But it did happen to me again, and this time in broad daylight. About a year later I was walking during summer break to my boyfriend's house a mile away. I was about three blocks from his house when a car pulled over to the wrong side of the road. The driver got out and grabbed me by the waist, attempting to pull and push me into his car. Even though this was before I learned that you should never let an attacker get you to another location, all at once I thought to myself, *Are you f**king kidding me?! You are NOT getting me into your car!* And just like that, there it was again—another attack and another scream. Certainly somebody would come out of their house and rescue me. Certainly somebody would drive by and see this guy trying to grab me. Nobody came. I felt like this was the story of my life: I couldn't rely on anybody to help me. I always had to do it myself—always alone.

I screamed my survivor scream, and he let go of me and drove off. There was no time to be still and wonder what to do—he could come back. I ran to the nearest house and pounded on the door. Nobody answered. I decided to make a run for it to my boyfriend's house. A block away, a car with a young couple in it pulled over and said they had seen me leaving their parents' house (the door I had knocked on), and wondered what I wanted. I told them what happened to me and they drove me to safety.

I wonder a lot about what would have happened to me in both of those scenarios if I hadn't fought back. For now I can only call it attempted abduction. I don't know if it would have meant rape, enslavement, being trafficked, or death. I do know that a little part of me died with each of those attacks. A little part of me believed these kinds of traumatic events were par for the course in my life. The world wasn't safe, people weren't safe, and I only had myself. I was officially the loneliest person on the planet.

At this point, anxiety, fear, and panic ruled my life even though I was still a teenager. I remember once when I went to the doctor and told her I was having trouble breathing. She looked at my suntan and indicated that I must have had too much sun. Unfortunately, she didn't pick up on the fact that I was suffering from anxiety and panic attacks. There were many more breakdowns in communication with doctors in the coming years, being misdiagnosed and mis-understood. I was having more and more suicidal thoughts but kept them under wraps because I didn't need anybody thinking I was weirder than they already did. All of my friends seemed to be happy and enjoying life, so I kept my dark secret in a desperate hope to fit in.

When I was a junior in high school I started self-medicating, drinking on the weekends, smoking, and taking drugs, mostly pills at that time. For some reason, I took uppers, which was the last thing my already anxious body needed. I really didn't care if I lived or died and often put myself in dangerous situations: partying with people I didn't know or trust, being in cars with boys who drove carelessly, walking around drunk at night, being present at drug deals, and other thoughtless activities. Slowly the dimmer switch was gradually being turned lower; I felt that soon my light would be completely out.

My life was gray, all color removed. All meaning was gone, and the only task I focused on was escape. All I cared about was getting through each day until I would turn eighteen and could move out of the house. As young adults often do, I assumed that moving out of the house would cure all of my woes, and I would be endlessly happy because I had escaped the wrath of my family. But that endless happiness continued to elude me even while in my own apartment. Yes, I felt an initial sense of freedom and happiness to be on my own, but that soon faded, as I still faced my personal struggles. I didn't know who I was as a person, and I stayed in survival mode because that was all I knew. My unhealthy behaviors continued. Instead of going to school and being miserable, I had a job and was miserable.

In my early twenties, I progressed from alcohol and pills to cocaine and got involved in abusive relationships with men, because again, that was all I knew. I was a mess, but because I was an expert survivor, I always got up the next day and somehow managed to keep up my charade. I didn't know I was living a lie. I didn't know how much I was suffering inside from the traumas, anxieties, fears, and drugs. From the outside I appeared to be fine, even having a great time, until my lies and self-abuse eventually caught up with me, manifesting emotional and physical illnesses.

I didn't know at the time that I was getting a big wake-up call. I wish I had, but I didn't. It seems to me everyone gets their wake-up call one way or another—a car crash, the death of a loved one, the loss of a home or a job, or, in my case, a devastating illness.

It began one day innocently enough. I was walking through a mall when I suddenly felt strange. I could not pinpoint how I felt because it really wasn't translatable into words—it was just an unsettling, "off" feeling in my body. It was so peculiar and overwhelming for me that I decided to leave the mall immediately and drive back home.

At the time, I was about twenty-five years old and had recently dealt with two bouts of mononucleosis (mono), something I'd previously had in high school. I was no longer doing drugs at this point; I'd quit the night I met my husband-to-be, when I was twenty-four. Scott was a bright light in my world, and I just didn't feel like I needed to do those things. He wasn't the type of person to indulge, so it was quite easy to quit pills and cocaine. I hadn't given up the alcohol yet, but soon my body wouldn't allow me to drink anymore.

I had quit my job as an associate producer at a TV station/production company, being too sick with mono to continue. Slowly I recuperated enough to work temp jobs to pay the bills and get my feet wet again before looking for full-time work in my field. However, I never got to that point, as my health quickly declined.

I had odd symptoms, such as hot flashes and night sweats, tinnitus, utter physical exhaustion, brain fog, interrupted sleep, bad memory, a sore throat and swollen glands, the inability to make a decision, sore muscles, intolerance to exercise, headaches, muscle weakness, and additional strange symptoms. I could no longer even have a glass of wine, as I would immediately get a stomachache and become dizzy. *How could I be having all these symptoms at such a young age?* At its worst, I couldn't get out of bed, and I will never forget the day when I was so weak Scott had to carry me to the bathroom. I had hit rock bottom and felt humiliated and defeated.

This was no longer a case of mono, and I felt lost, confused, and frustrated without a clear diagnosis. Remember, this was before the internet, so I was left with only books, magazines, daytime talk shows, and random strangers to research for clues and answers. I met with doctors and specialists, and had every medical test available at the time: extensive blood work, EKG, MRI, EEG, allergy testing, and more. One diagnosis after the next was tossed around, like Lyme disease or multiple sclerosis, filling me with vast amounts of fear.

At one point I found a book that said an overgrowth of yeast was the cause, so I followed a special diet and did feel a bit better—for a while. I thought I was losing my mind as the symptoms got stranger and more pronounced. My cognitive abilities were failing, and sometimes I couldn't walk straight. At this point I was housebound.

In desperation I contacted a neurologist, the best in the state. He gave me all the regular tests, and I did fine on them. Finally he sat me down and said, "You are the sickest person I know and I have no idea what is wrong with you." I will always love and appreciate him for his honesty, but it was quite difficult and scary to hear this from a highly regarded doctor. I really wanted a diagnosis and didn't want to leave his office without one, so when I pushed him he said, "chronic fatigue syndrome (CFS)."

Chronic fatigue syndrome was a catchall label for patients who had a range of similar yet strange symptoms and needed a diagnosis. It was the new buzzword in the health world at the time and slowly became a widespread epidemic. He wanted to start me on antidepressants, but I told him, "I'm not depressed!"

In all honesty, by that time I *was* depressed, and I was sick and tired of being sick and tired.

I felt defeated. Here was this well-respected doctor giving me medication for people who had depression—what did that mean? Did it mean my symptoms were all in my head? Could I be crazy? But I knew it wasn't all in my head; I had physical symptoms!

The kind and patient doctor wrote me a prescription for Prozac, saying that the medication would take about thirty days to kick in. I left feeling confused but happy, in a way, just to have a pill I could take. I was ready to do anything to feel better. If the pills didn't help all of my strange symptoms, at least maybe I would no longer feel tired of being sick.

I filled the prescription immediately, and as soon as I got home, opened my first bottle of little half-green, half-cream capsules. I took one and forgot about it, looking forward to day thirty when perhaps I would be cured. What happened next was incredible: I didn't have to wait thirty days or even thirty minutes. In just about twenty minutes after ingesting my first Prozac, I felt my brain "turn on." I felt alive, and I felt strange surges of electricity in my head. No doctor except my current one believes me when I tell this story. "Impossible!" the others say. "It takes weeks for the medication to work!" They thought it was "all in my head"—and it *was*. My brain was finally waking up from a long slumber.

Feeling alert and turned on for the first time in

my life, I told Scott, "Let's go to the m
I think his jaw hit the floor, because I ha
housebound for so long. In retrospect, I believe
my brain was so lacking in neurotransmitters that
it was like a sponge soaking them up; and when
it finally got what it so desperately needed, it
performed the way it should. (Neurotransmitters
are chemicals that cells produce to send signals
between your nerve cells. You have probably
heard of many neurotransmitters, such as serotonin, dopamine, epinephrine, and histamine.
Low serotonin levels are present in people with
depression.) Even though I was feeling well
enough to get out, I was still suffering from
physical symptoms. The medication simply acted
as a boost of energy to get me off the sofa; it
didn't address the underlying, root problem.

Now that I could get out of the house, I
decided I should see a psychiatrist because,
apparently, everything was in my head. I made
an appointment with one, and was expecting to
walk into his office and see the traditional sofa or
chaise lounge where I would lie down. I guess I
had watched too many movies—his office didn't
look like that at all. He had an ordinary office
chair for me to sit in, which did not make me
happy—not so much from disappointment but
because I was still sick and tired, and needed a
sofa I could curl up or stretch out on. I decided
to sit on the floor instead, so I could stretch out

nd move around more. He did not like that, initiating a conversation with me about how it was affecting him. I found a new psychiatrist.

The second time around, I chose a woman, and she *did* have a nice comfy sofa for me and conversed with me in a much less clinical way, which was more to my liking. An important first lesson I learned: Choose your healthcare providers wisely. Pick somebody you are comfortable with and who listens to you.

Unfortunately, my brain's euphoria on Prozac didn't last long. A couple of months into my prescription, I started to not feel so well again, and my psychiatrist gave me a larger dose. I felt good for a while until I went down again. Up and down again. Over and over. By this time I was also taking antianxiety medication, so I had a nice cocktail, with my psychiatrist acting as the bartender. She would ramp up my dose until I maxed out and then announce that I needed to start on a different antidepressant.

Over the years, I tried many different meds, including Prozac, Paxil, Zoloft, Effexor, Wellbutrin, and Xanax. This dizzying dance went on for a very long time—try a medication, ramp up, max out, change to another medication— until I lost all sense of myself and couldn't feel anything anymore. It was as if a blanket had been thrown over my head, blinding me and making it impossible to live with any sense of normalcy.

I continued therapy with my psychiatrist and I was still a mental mess. Some days I would see her when I was happy and have nothing to talk about, and then I would choose not to see her when I was feeling low, because I felt like a failure. I eventually dropped her, as it became clear she wasn't helping me. Our relationship had become transactional—it was all about renewing my prescriptions, which I realized I didn't need her to do as long as I had my primary doctor. However, leaving my psychiatrist was a big part of the roller-coaster ride with my meds, because my primary doctor didn't really care about my mental health. Again, it was a transactional deal; I would show up and tell her what she wanted to hear, and she would renew my prescription.

From my experience, this type of automated healthcare can be disastrous. I've come to firmly believe that if you are taking these types of medications, you need to support your health-care by being in some sort of effective talk therapy, whether with a counselor, psychologist, or psychiatrist—a professional you can trust who cares about your mental health and will listen to you, creating a program that's tailored to your needs. In the beginning, I hadn't learned to advocate for my health; I hadn't learned to question or ask for the care I needed—to find a doctor or a talk therapist who could help me beyond the medications they prescribed. Whatever they prescribed, I believed I had to have it, and that was it.

With my mental health spiraling down, I decided on my own to take myself off medication. I was tired of popping pills and feeling either extremely numb like a robot or the opposite: jumpy like a wind-up doll. When I decided to stop taking the meds, I had no clue that people should never just stop taking antidepressants on their own; they need to be weaned off slowly. I went cold turkey—big mistake. I spent the next couple of weeks being the most miserable I had ever been in my life. My brain would deliver explosive electric shocks, and I was left a shell of myself on the sofa, unable to do anything at all. The slightest bit of light or noise was like torture. I wished it would all end. I wished I had a gun so I could shoot myself in the head—that's how volatile and dangerous it got for me. Mental health is not to be taken lightly or as a joke. It isn't so much that I didn't want to be alive but that I didn't want to be alive like that.

Each day I woke up hoping that my suffering would be over and that my brain chemistry would be back to some sense of normal. I lived in agony for weeks. Going off medication on my own was probably one of the worst decisions I have ever made and one I would never do again; I'm incredibly thankful that I survived it. But I did learn a crucial lesson: just because our mental health can't be seen like a bodily wound, such as a cut or a broken bone, doesn't mean it isn't imperative that it be taken care of properly.

Having survived, though, I'll be the first to say it was nice to be free of the controlling antidepressant and antianxiety medications once they were finally out of my system. And by freeing myself from their hold, I reached a radical decision that if I was going to feel bad, I wanted to feel bad naturally. I would find a way to live unmedicated, but I had to get serious about how I was going to live my life. I knew I still needed help and I was still suffering from symptoms of CFS (chronic fatigue syndrome), but I wanted to find another way to healing and wellness. I made a promise to myself to try some alternative and natural therapies, and I made my first appointment with an acupuncturist. After all, I had nothing to lose.

In truth I had everything to lose—my capacity for happiness or even my life—but by radically changing the course of how I treated and thought of my health, I gradually gained my life back. I had a chance to finally live as a whole being.

I hope that reading my story and having a picture of where I have been, where the struggle started, and how it manifested gives you inspiration about what's achievable. You have the power within to transform and heal your life just as I did; you just need to learn *how*. Therefore, let's shift to how I learned to heal myself, how I got off and stayed off antidepressant and antianxiety medications, how I stopped self-medicating through unhealthy behaviors, and how I began living a full and rewarding life.

Once I decided to reach out to the alternative health community, I consulted with more than thirty different types of healers: acupuncturists, naturopaths, herbalists, homeopaths, psychics, shamans, medical intuitives, Reiki practitioners, astrologers, and more. Some of the things I tried were downright odd, but this is what a desperately ill person does. And I learned something about my mind, body, and spirit from each healer. All the therapies I experienced eventually gave me the framework to curate an effective and holistic wellness program. Through trial and error, research, recommendations, and practice, I discovered the essentials that have become the basis for what this book teaches.

Learning to heal myself through natural means, I came to the profound realization that my healing path is a lifelong process. The motivation and desire to be happy and healthy in the most natural way possible stemmed from an authentic part of myself, and it is from this authenticity that real change lasts forever. I also came to discover that healing does not have to be expensive, dramatic, or complicated. Healing can be inexpensive, drama free, and simple.

By "simple" I do not mean easy; though I don't consider my process difficult by any means, it does take dedication. Most people are looking for a quick fix, or a pill to make their life better, or the next fad diet, or a guru who will change their life forever. People look everywhere outside themselves in order to avoid facing the truth of what is inside. I want to tell you that there is power in simplicity and there is strength in building a foundation from within.

I am asking for your time and dedication to do the work. **When you do this work and follow the practices, you are declaring to the Universe, "I want this; I am ready."** The Universe will respond in kind. It is in your actions that you speak volumes, and I will tell you from firsthand experience that this works. I teach a healing process involving your entire being—mind, body, and spirit. For me, Spirit is not used in a religious context. It is a place deep within me that knows all on a soul level—a healing place within the soul. But Spirit can mean whatever you want it to mean.

Whether you want to be happy and stay happy, find relief from depression and anxiety, or create change in some other aspect of your life, this process will stir the pot and give you oppor- tunities to take action and make real changes. It is important to remember that change and the answers we are looking for often show up in ways we don't expect. I will teach you to go with the flow, allowing these experiences to show up in your life and handling them like the old soul that you are.

In this book, I am going to teach you an easy-to-follow, gentle healing program that can change your life—provided you dedicate time each and every day to it. There is no right or wrong about how much time you give, as that is up to you to personalize. This healing foundation I offer will only work for you if you dedicate time and attention to it, because it is in your *action* that you open the gateway to change.

It is said that teachers teach what they need to learn. It is also said that when the student is ready, the teacher will show up. I have spent my life up until this very moment learning in depth what is contained in this book, and it is my offering to you—to help guide you on your way. I have never considered myself a teacher but more of a friend who shares information to help others. And you have bravely shown up, so let us begin.

1

The Unmedicated
Program:
A New Healing
Foundation

W hen we think of medication in the traditional sense, we think about pills taken on a daily basis to provide relief from a specific ailment. Our doctor writes us a prescription for what ails us and we begin the regimen. Normally we accept the medication without question, because we fully believe it will make us well and we trust our doctor with our health. In many cases, this belief is warranted. In these situations, the medication has a direct intent and use, and taken for a period of time, it can give much-needed relief and healing.

Unmedicated offers an alternative, holistic path for people who want to heal themselves from the crippling effects that excessive reliance on medications such as antidepressants can create in the body, mind, and spirit. I hear too often from my friends, colleagues, or those who write to me through DailyOM, "I'm suffering on medication." This book is for them and for you—for anyone who wants to be their healthiest. I want to provide a new, gentle option—a guide based on the assumption that you know best the roots of what debilitates you and prevents you from living fully. I'm a big believer in taking your health into your own hands, which really means taking your life into your own hands.

You must advocate for your own health because nobody else is going to. You must practice being inquisitive, informed, and proactive. At first it may be challenging and maybe even intimidating to question your doctor. I know firsthand because I had to learn to find the courage to speak up. Now, whenever I am offered medication, I always ask these two questions:

1. Is there a lifestyle change I can make first to avoid taking this medication?

2. Is there an underlying, root cause of the condition?

It isn't always possible to find the answers, but I always investigate first, and being informed leaves me feeling empowered rather than deflated. When you decide to really advocate for your own health, it means having a conversation with your doctor and then researching on your own. I check the website of the pharmaceutical company to read side effects and studies, I check with friends to see if they have taken the medication, and I look online for any negative feedback from other people who have taken it.

I do the same thing when exploring an alternative: Is there an herbal or homeopathic remedy? A lifestyle or dietary change I can make? For too long we have given our power away to our doctors. If you are fortunate enough to have a family doctor who has known you well and for a long time, count yourself lucky. Most people have multiple doctors for different ailments and have zero personal connection with their caregivers. Because we often lack a relationship with our doctors, there is a disconnect, and we simply take the prescription order and fill it; we assume that is what is best for us. Maybe the prescription *is* best for you, but you owe it to yourself to find out why.

There are other types of medication, though, besides pharmaceuticals—the type we use to self-medicate, such as addictive behaviors involving food, social media, work, sex, gambling, alcohol, isolation, and illicit drugs. We tend to self-medicate to numb ourselves of an emotional pain, past abuse, or trauma; we want to protect ourselves from the deep pain we don't want to feel. I know this from personal experience.

All of these types of behaviors throw a blanket over us so we no longer have to feel our feelings or participate in life fully, with an open heart. We are so brilliant as a human species that we have a built-in protection system to keep us from harm, and each of us chooses what seems to fit appropriately. Any behavior you engage in to make you not feel your emotional pain could be considered self-medicating.

Slowly, over time, these behaviors take hold, become addictive, and take over your existence, often without your recognizing it. We know about the destructive habits of illicit drug use, but

39

we may not notice how the behavior of isolation can become detrimental to our well-being. When isolation becomes a firmly rooted belief in your life, shielding yourself from friendships and relationships, it can silently evolve into a deep fear that prevents you from ever leaving your house. Because there is no blood test needed for this, we pass it off as just wanting to be alone.

Or maybe you enjoy your wine each day after work but don't realize when, at some point, it shifts into *needing* the wine each day rather than just enjoying it—the point where one glass becomes two or three. Or perhaps you feel bored, which leads you to spend countless hours online, surfing the internet with no real purpose or value. You don't recognize that the boredom and isolation are signs of depression; you don't recognize that getting tipsy or drunk each day allows you to ignore feelings that desperately want to be acknowledged.

All of these physical and emotional behaviors and actions derail you from living your best and most fulfilled life. You don't mean to do it, and you aren't a bad person or a failure for taking up these behaviors. Like I shared in my own story, by continuing to ignore and numb my feelings, these behaviors never went away but instead manifested as debilitating illness, depression, and anxiety. Fortunately, all of my self-medicating behaviors changed and I am healthy now, and you can do the same thing if you take the time and dedicate yourself to improving your wellness.

The Unmedicated Program

So how did I learn to heal myself? How did I get off antidepressants and antianxiety meds? How did I stop self-medicating and begin living a full, rewarding life?

What follows is very important, and each topic is vital to the program. At first, you may think it is a lot to take in and do each day, but once you get the hang of it, it will become second nature. Time and practice will make it easier. Remember: You're about to embark on a journey to health and wellness, and I believe that's worth your attention. The benefits will more than justify the means.

My Unmedicated Program establishes a healing foundation built upon four pillars of action—your go-to items and practices to follow. Under each pillar are two to three essential action steps along with some optional steps you can take to enhance your experience. The four pillars are:

1. Clear Your Mind
2. Nurture Your Spirit
3. Strengthen Your Body
4. Find Your Tribe

As you progress through the book and I explain each pillar, you will recognize how they all work together, laying the foundation for the new "home" of health and wellness you will live in and from. Each pillar builds upon the last one, so don't skip a step, or your new home will crumble. It is also important to work the pillars in the order I give them, although the optional steps can be done at any time. All the pillars have specific functions that work together in unison for the common goal—to foster, nurture, and sustain a healthier and happier you.

You may be wondering how long this program will take, and that is a valid question; it is not one I can answer, however. Each person will set his or her own personal timeline. You see, we are all unique human beings with different chemistry and in different stages of health. One person might be able to make significant changes in one month, but somebody else might take six months or a year. It would be disrespectful and dangerous of me to rush your individual process; therefore, I won't discuss a timeline in this book. How can you put a time limit on your health? This isn't the twenty-four-hour flu; this is your lifelong well-being. It deserves all of the attention and time you can give it. Respect for your individual healing process is vital.

Each pillar should be worked for at least a

week before you add on the next pillar. It will be different for everybody, so this is where you need to listen to your own body and check in with yourself. As you work the program, your intuitive skills will sharpen, becoming an easier and more natural wellspring to access. If you ever feel overwhelmed, you can back off a bit, be gentle, and stay where you are for a while before moving on.

Also, there are many practices in my program that will benefit you for years to come. In particular you can revisit the writing work over and over again, and each time you do, you will find a deeper layer to travel. There really is no end to the depth you can visit when it comes to your feelings. Once you have spent quality time with each pillar, you will see how they move together like a dance—and eventually, I promise you, you will enjoy the dance.

The Importance of Taking Action

In order to save myself, I came up with a series of actions to cause a shift. It is through these actions that I can now maintain a healthy balance in my life. Therefore, my program involves a promise *from you* to take action every day. The process will not work if you just read the book and put it down. You need to work the program, take daily action, and stay accountable to yourself.

Thoughts alone will not change your life, but adding actions into the equation will. To set up the shift and counterbalance addictions, negative thought patterns, and behaviors, you need to take physical action. Merely sitting on the sofa thinking good thoughts and making wishes is not good enough. Over the last ten years or so, the idea of manifesting by desiring what you want and focusing on it has become very popular. I do not at all disagree with this kind of belief but have learned it leaves out a vital step: taking action based on thoughts. The thought or desire is a source of inspiration and motivation for you and is a wonderful, sincere feeling to have. Let it fuel your energy and commitment to go to the next level and achieve your dreams.

All of the actions throughout this book are a declaration to the Universe that you are ready to start a shift. Empower yourself with action, and the Universe will respond and cocreate with you. Everything that occurs in your life affects your whole self—your emotional self, soul, mind, and physical body. The steps I have set up in this book affect all of those parts of you— they interconnect and integrate to help create healing. It is important that all of these parts are addressed, as you cannot simply address one and expect all to be well. They work together as a team for you, and the Universe is part of your team!

Because I have suffered from depression and anxiety for so much of my life, it has turned into a constant manifestation that I don't want to really be in this life. Depression put a blanket on everything so that a part of me said, "Let's not participate in life, because it is not safe." As a child growing up I learned that my spiritual and emotional bodies were not acceptable, so I learned to silence them. As a result, my physical body could not function as it should, and that showed up in many harmful ways. My brain and nervous system literally changed their configuration, and depression and anxiety were the result.

Because my inner voice communicated very loudly to me that I was not good enough, I had to take contrary action. I needed to teach my brain a different way of dealing with its reality. In order to rewire myself and get my spiritual, emotional, and physical body working together again, I needed a set of contrary, healing actions. I had to take charge of my brain, my health, and my life, quieting the harmful and sabo- taging voice while retraining my brain and body in ways that fostered care, compassion, and love.

I would like to add a gentle reminder to all of you courageous souls who are willing to take action and do this work: please know that when you choose to do this deep and powerful work, emotions and memories will rise to the surface and make themselves known to you. When this happens, please take extra care of yourself. However, this is not the time to drop your program; this is the time to stay dedicated to it, because the work in this book will help you get through your issues in the most loving way possible.

You may experience emotional dreams; or a simple conversation with somebody may bring up past pain and issues for you. Try to turn your thinking into realizing that these upheavals are positive rather than a reason to go into a downward spiral. This is not the time to think you are a failure; your emotional pain needs to be brought to the surface so it can be looked at, examined, and acknowledged in order to heal. Long-buried feelings hiding in the darkness cannot be healed; it is only in the light, where you bravely look at your pain, that healing takes place.

You will not be left to flounder on your own, as you are never really alone. The Universe is here to support you; this book is here to support you. Remember your friends and loved ones. Cherish the opportunity you now have to take action and become a person in charge of your life. No major life shift should be decided on a whim, and I want you to feel fully supported in whatever decision you make for your well-being.

I believe that the content in this book can serve

anybody whether you are medicated or not. Even if you choose to stay on your medication after reading this book and working the program, you will still find helpful support and enhancements to your healthcare routine. This program can be a wonderful foundation and guide for anybody wanting to improve the quality of their life.

2

Pillar One:
Clear Your Mind

This pillar is the foundation for all of the others to follow. Its main practices are meditation and spending quality time connecting in nature. Both of these steps help clear your mind, which is vital to this work. When I talk about clearing your mind, I am not referring to erasing anything or forcing anything to go away. Clearing your mind involves creating a relaxed, calm, and empty space within your mind so you may fill it up with the good stuff, such as worrying less, being more in the present moment, allowing negativity to wash over you, and not letting the little things be a bother. These rewards and more are waiting for you.

Pillar One will teach you how to dial back and slow down your brain. When you slip into a nice, relaxed state such as a light meditation or daydream, your brain enters what is referred to as the alpha state—a state where you slow down, think less, and are relaxed. This is the gateway to your subconscious mind before entering the theta state, which is the state of mind where you are in deep meditation.

When you are in theta for a short time each day, it allows you to access what is normally hidden while you are in your everyday doing/thinking state of mind, also known as the beta state. Theta waves get past your thinking mind and allow your daydreams to come forward, accessing what your soul desires. This process reaches different centers in your brain that you simply don't access during your regular waking hours in beta.

When you don't regularly take time to slow down your brain activity, you keep your conscious brain and ego in the driver's seat. They are protecting you from your pain, so you react to them and indulge in unwise decisions, such as addictive behavior and staying in depression. When you access your deeper, higher state of being, it is like making an announcement that you are ready and willing to do the work. You want to know what peace and, ultimately, good health feel like.

Taking time to clear your mind each day will make you more focused during your regular activities; research shows that mindfulness improves attention and memory. When you take the time to be mindful, slow down, and allow your brain to be quiet, you are, in essence, training it, working your mental muscles. When you have practiced meditation to a point where you can achieve a high level of concentration, you are making significant improvements. Along with attention and memory, many people also receive other physical benefits, such as lower blood pressure. In my opinion, meditation really is the best "medicine" available; there is no downside!

Ideally, you should clear your mind on a daily basis, and this is something you can strive to work toward. I believe it is better to take some time each day rather than doing it for longer periods only a few days a week. As you practice over time, it will become a healthy habit your body will want and crave, like a dog craves that moment you return home from work. Reward the dog and give it what it wants. When you don't do it, it is like breaking an agreement with yourself, so take the time even if you only have a few minutes a day.

There are 720 minutes available to you in a twelve-hour day, and most people are awake for longer than twelve hours. Make the time to find ten to twenty minutes a day by spending less time online or on your phone. It is amazing how much time we waste once we take the time to notice. This is your health—make the time.

Step 1: Meditate
(Five to Seven Days a Week)

The word *meditation* can be an uncomfortable one for many—a bit of a mystery—and perhaps it brings up some questions, and maybe even fear. We often see images of people in meditation sitting on shiny cushions, wearing silk robes and mala beads from India, and in full lotus pose, their legs seemingly tangled in an impossible position. Whew! If this works for you and is your preferred route, fantastic! But for most people, it isn't their reality.

To meditate you don't need to go to a foreign country; buy special clothing; sit in full lotus position; or have beads, incense, jewelry, or a meditation cushion. You only need to bring yourself and your willingness to take time each day to be still and quiet your mind. That is all. It is up to you whether you want to add on to your experience with accessories that can support your meditation practice.

The purpose of meditation is to clear your mind and be in the present moment. I liken it to brushing your teeth: you wouldn't leave your house in the morning without brushing your teeth, so why would you start your day without clearing your mind? We usually have the same excuses: "I don't have time" or "I'm too busy today," or any number of other justifications. But those days in particular are when you need it the most, because meditation will give you what you need to get *through* your day. It creates the necessary space for you to be ready to meet your day. For example, if you face a busy day full of meetings, you will want to enter those meetings with a clear and peaceful head space, which meditation provides.

Earlier, I mentioned the term *mindfulness,* which, along with meditation, is becoming mainstream. Mindfulness is a form of meditation:

a state of being in which you are consciously mindful of what you are doing and feeling in any given moment. A great example of mindfulness is how it is taught to young children. When my son was in kindergarten, the teachers brought the children outside to sit in a circle and asked them to close their eyes and just be. The teachers asked: "What do you hear right now? What do you smell? What do you sense?" The children would sit for about five minutes simply noticing, using all of their senses except their eyesight. In another exercise, they were given a carrot to eat and, again, with their eyes closed, were asked to concentrate on that carrot in their mouth: "What does it taste like? Do you notice the crunching sound? How long do you need to chew?" This is the basis of mindfulness—being in the present moment right where you are.

You can see how mindfulness is a big part of meditation, especially when you are starting out, because you use it to simply notice any distraction that is happening around you and then allow the distraction to wash away.

I stumbled upon meditation during my long illness while in my midtwenties. I was so ill and depressed that I was desperate to try anything. While browsing in a local metaphysical/New Thought store, I noticed a display with CDs that claimed to be "relaxing." The photos on the CD covers looked so nice that I decided to buy a couple to try out. Once I was home, I settled into a comfy chair and floated away for forty minutes. I was struck by how relaxed I was at the end of the CD, and I felt clearheaded and seemed to have more energy. I also noticed that I had drifted away but was not asleep—I had entered a complete state of relaxation.

Because it made me feel much better, I vowed to listen each day (or at least five days a week) and committed to this practice. This was my early journey into starting a meditation practice; I just didn't know it yet! What it did for me was create a commitment to "sitting" each day and listening to the meditation music. I tried to pick the same time each day, and I found that when the time was near, I would instinctively know it was time to sit and listen, without an outside reminder. This became such an enjoyable time of my day, and I noticed the healing benefits. I could make decisions more easily, my reaction to others' negativity wasn't met with negativity, and I felt as if I literally had more space in my head. I felt calmer in general, and the world didn't seem so overwhelming after all. There was also a little more spring in my step after my sessions, which I couldn't achieve any other way.

Meditation music was my gateway to silent sitting meditation. For me it worked out well to start with baby steps before getting into some serious, extended, quiet meditation time. Once I was ready to explore meditation in a deeper way, I took the leap, letting go of my music time and diving into traditional meditation.

When I first started my new practice, it was too painful to sit in an upright position with my back straight. (In my music sessions, I was in a reclining chair.) I had a weak core and a weak back, making it extremely uncomfortable for me to sit in the traditional cross-legged or lotus position. So I began my meditation experience lying on my bed, which is exactly what every meditation teacher says *not* to do. (I did it anyway.) I easily found myself slipping into a relaxed state. Afterward I would "wake up" and look at the clock in astonishment; I had always meditated for exactly twenty minutes.

Die-hard meditators would not call this meditation, but it felt good to me, so I kept it up each day for a few months. What mattered was that I was doing it, not that I was doing it the "right" way. I didn't know it then, but I was creating the foundation for my evolving practice, forming a habit of taking the time to sit (or lie down) each day in silence. It didn't matter whether I was doing it right or wrong; I was doing it and feeling good because of it.

Eventually I felt the tug to leave my bed and started to sit on a chair or sofa to meditate. I would make sure my feet were grounded on the floor and place pillows behind my back for support, creating a good, comfortable sitting position with a straight spine. The transition from lying down to sitting was hard at first, but I kept with it until it became my new normal.

I would be lying if I said that meditation came easily to me. It didn't. I have a mind that runs fast, always processing, always active, always trying to figure things out. I have been told that I have a "great brain" and it serves me well in life, but it is also hard to quiet down. Meditation is hard for those of us with busy brains, but it also gives us the most benefit, as it is a wonderful way to slow our brains down.

I remember reading meditation books that advised envisioning thoughts floating by like clouds, letting them easily pass by. But with my mind, I would imagine cute cloud bunnies and angels, or think about the sun and then the beach.

Because it was tough in the beginning, I thought that perhaps meditation wasn't for me. I was a failure at being still, and maybe I *did* need to go to India and find a guru. Determined not to give up, though, I turned to guided meditation, with a person's voice guiding me through the steps to slowing down my mind. I found that this helped tremendously in giving me the twenty to thirty minutes I needed to turn off my thinking and relax. I also experimented with different teachers, as some voices resonated with me more than others, and I tried music meditations designed to create the same effect.

Another aspect of meditation that I came to slowly learn is that almost any repetitive action can be turned into a meditation, such as doing the dishes in silence or walking in silence alone, without interruption. I say this to save you any anguish you may feel if you are like me and don't connect immediately with traditional sitting meditation.

Now I love meditation so much that I have even created my own series of guided meditations and an extensive online course for my readers. If you are interested, you can find these at DailyOM.com. My guided meditation CD/download entitled *Eagle Meditation* is a wonderful, relaxing, guided journey that is good for beginners in particular.

Here are two of my meditations you can practice.

BASIC BEGINNER'S MEDITATION

- Put on some loose, comfortable clothing that will not bind while you are sitting. Turn off phones, the TV, the radio, and anything else that may interrupt your quiet time.

- Try to pick a time that allows you to meditate at or near the same time every day. Ideally, morning meditation is best, but you can do it at any time during the day. Of course, if you cannot meditate at the same time each day, this should not hinder you. It is better to do it anytime than not at all.

- Advanced practitioners meditate twenty to thirty (or more) minutes per day, but you only need ten minutes a day to see and feel results. Thirty minutes sounds like a long time to sit in silence, but this will soon become easy for you.

- Start by preparing your meditation area every time before you sit to begin your practice. A light dusting or cleaning up of the area helps to state your intention. You're telling the Universe, "I am ready." If you have a candle or incense or a bell or singing bowl, use those items now to signal the start of your practice. However, these items are not necessary.

- Get into the position that will work best for you and start to relax. Place your hands on your thighs or knees, and open your palms upward toward the ceiling.

Take a giant, deep breath and let it out. Set your intention that this is now your meditation time. By doing this, you are declaring to the Universe that you want this—you are taking an action to facilitate change in your life.

• For the first week of your practice, just sit quietly and breathe; get used to the idea of performing this action, taking the time, and setting your intention. Breathe for ten minutes, focusing on your breaths in and out.

• Make no judgment about what happens during this time. Many people can't quiet their minds at first, so don't feel bad if you are one of them. You will think about your day, your shopping list, the chores you have to do, and the work that needs to be done. Your mind may wander, and that is okay. As soon as you realize your mind has started thinking, release the thoughts and just breathe.

• Congratulations, you have just meditated!

(Note: Some people like to add mala beads to this basic practice. This is a string of beads, usually between eighteen to one hundred and eight beads; as you hold the string in your hands, you slowly run your fingers over each bead, using them as a natural counting device. Traditionally you would chant your "mantra" with the touch of each bead. You can buy mala beads or make your own. Again, this is not necessary; it is simply another tool.)

BEGINNER'S GUIDED MEDITATION

Another easy meditation for beginners is guided meditation, where a soothing voice guides you into a relaxed state and then takes you on a visual journey. Some visual journeys are simply for relaxation, and others can be for a specific purpose, such as healing emotional pain. For the purposes of my Unmedicated Program, it is important to practice stillness meditation before moving on to meditations that offer healing aspects. (Note: You can record the following steps using your own voice, or you can simply read them slowly. Feel free to put on some relaxing music to accompany your practice.)

- Take three big breaths in and out to release any tension you may be feeling.

- Sit comfortably and just notice any sounds around you, allowing them to wash through you. This is your time to focus on you—on relaxing, quieting your mind, and releasing all thoughts. Notice in your body where you are holding any tension. Squeeze those muscles and then release them. Allow your shoulders to drop away from your neck.

- Take some more deep breaths and roll your neck if it is comfortable for you to do so. If active thoughts keep coming to mind, simply acknowledge them and then send them along.

- Now imagine your body awash in a brilliant light. This light feels very relaxing to you; and with every breath in and out, you feel more and more relaxed and still. You feel peaceful and safe in a bubble of brilliant light.

- Sit in this relaxation as long as you wish. When you feel ready, wiggle your toes and stretch, coming back to your fully awakened state.

Our meditation experience is unique to each of us, and there is a meditation practice to suit everybody. What works for your best friend may not work for you. It took me a while to find my groove with meditation, and ultimately I found that I prefer guided meditations with music in the background, and then simple silence meditations of breathing and relaxing while in a seated position. Another tip: Try not to make your exploration of meditation too serious. Yes, it is important, but have fun experimenting with all of the different ways you can bring meditation into your life. Of all of the practices in this book, meditation is far and above the most important, so please take the time to find what works for you. If you don't like it, you won't do it, so find your perfect fit.

Step 2: Connect with Nature
(Five to Seven Days a Week)

Some of the most awe-inspiring moments of my life have occurred outdoors, in the presence of nature: witnessing an incredible moonrise from behind a hill, with the moon feeling close enough to jump on it; feeling the power of waves breaking at the beach, reminding me that nature is a powerful force; observing the silence of a summer night and staring at the stars, my mind filled with questions about where we came from; finding a magnificent tree that beckons me to sit beneath her.

When I was a young girl, I often felt that nature was my real best friend. I found so much comfort in the woods, among the mountains and lakes, and even in our own garden. When I was in nature, I knew that all would be all right; she was like a comfy blanket and teddy bear in my times of distress. To this day, I still get the same feelings, as if somebody is hugging me, letting me know that no matter what is worrying me, I can take a deep breath with Mother Nature and all will be well.

Mother Earth is a living meditation; her beauty is everywhere, boundless in her never-ending cycles of life. This is why I make time every day to connect with nature, even if it is only in my garden, knowing that I will slip easily into a calmer state there. Nature both energizes and grounds me, providing me with the perfect energetic attunement needed in that moment. The beauty of nature is that it is available to everybody; even those living in cities have many parks to choose from, and a small spot can become your special place to relax and connect. Nature wants to come forth—wants our connection. In turn we are nourished by its abundance.

There is really nothing that will bring you back to center within yourself faster than breathing fresh air and walking in a meadow, among the trees, or on a beach. But there is a difference between being *in* nature and being *with* nature.

When we are in nature, we notice her beauty and what she has to offer, perhaps by going for a hike; but when we are truly *with* nature, we become one with her. All at once we can feel her and notice how we are all connected. We are brought out of our own awareness of our daily life and grounded in something deeper and more meaningful. We are provided a peace and a unity with *all* life.

Take the time to go out on nature dates—sit on a rock, on a bench at a park, or under a tree: listen and breathe. You don't need to check your messages, text, or make a call. Just close your eyes and connect. This is how you get grounded; this is how you center your energy in your body. All at once your shoulders will drop and your body will relax. Mother Earth wants to connect with you; she has been waiting for you and will receive you lovingly in her heart if you just take the time to sit still.

I love nature so much—our great Mother Earth who really *is* our ultimate mother! Becoming more in tune with nature made me realize how we, as a species, treat the earth. When I was still taking my medication, I became aware that all of the medication we put into our bodies ends up back in the earth and in our water. I read articles that said cities were finding antidepressant medication in their water systems, and it frightened me. I didn't want to be a part of that if I could help it. I love the earth so much, and we only have this one planet to live on. I realized that I didn't want to do anything in my life to contribute to her demise. I used this knowledge as part of my motivation to become free of medications. It became very clear that I needed to care for Mother Earth as she cares for me. This is the wonderful thing about "lightbulb" moments: we never know when or what will boost us onto the trajectory of a new and healthier path.

What are we doing to our planet—our home—and what can I do to help? These questions really lit a fire in me to take care of my body in the best possible way naturally, so I didn't add to the pharmaceuticals that were ending up in our resources. Part of living on this planet is being a good steward of the land, acting for the whole of humanity, and not acting selfishly. For a long time I struggled whenever I had to take an antibiotic or another pill, as I knew where it would eventually end up. If I could be one less person adding to this pollution, I wanted to do something about it.

As with all things, there must be balance, and knowing that I was aware of the issue and doing the best job I could was a good start. Communing and connecting with nature enhanced my awareness and made me fall deeply in love with Mother Earth—I wanted to protect and care for her so that she, too, could be healthy and whole.

How I wanted to treat and heal my body became a reflection of how I wanted to treat and heal our Earth.

The ways I try to help heal our Earth are:

- Not using pesticides in my garden or toxic cleaners in my home
- Growing a garden
- Planting trees and flowers
- Investigating how to get and care for a beehive
- Donating money to organizations that work to heal the planet
- Recycling whenever possible
- Writing to companies and organizations about how they can reduce their waste
- Picking up garbage when I'm out on a walk or a hike
- Cutting down on water waste and researching alternative energy sources
- Mentioning to my friends what I am doing and why it is important to me

There are no how-to instructions to practice your nature dates; you simply create time each day to be in nature. There are infinite possibilities, so make it personal and true to *you*. The goal is to simply do it, just like meditation, and build this rewarding and health-promoting habit. You will find some ideas in the optional steps that follow. Find what speaks to you or come up with your own wonderful ideas.

Optional Steps

CREATE AN ALTAR TO ENHANCE YOUR MEDITATION

Starting a meditation practice can be difficult at first—there is a reason it is called a "practice"! However, once you begin to feel the effects of meditation in your life, I promise you won't miss a day. It can become like a hobby, and you may find yourself buying a special pillow or a gemstone to enhance your experience. As I wrote earlier, it isn't necessary, but personalizing your practice may be a next step in tending to, caring for, and deepening your practice.

When you start a new hobby, it is natural to want to improve your skill and make the time you spend engaged in it more enjoyable. In regard to meditation, another step is to create a small (or large) altar. Again, it isn't necessary, but it is a wonderful reminder for you to meditate each day. When I see my altar, I am immediately drawn to meditate if I haven't already. I am also reminded of the relaxed feelings I have after I do.

Over time my altar collection has grown to include gemstones, feathers, rocks, and other bits of nature. I lovingly place each item on my altar along with a candle. My first altar was a hand-painted coffee table from India. Each day, I took time to tend to my altar by rearranging and replacing objects, lighting incense and candles, dusting the table, and placing flowers or herbs from my garden on it. My altar took on an energy of its own as I tended to it each day. I didn't know at the time that I was slowly creating a sacred place for my meditation practice. We were getting to know each other through a sacred dance—I would make a move by placing an object on the altar, and the altar would let me know intuitively where the object should be placed, or if the object shouldn't be on the altar at all. It was a reciprocating relationship of feeling and knowing.

The day eventually came when my altar signaled to me that it was time that I sit before it. I really adore how Spirit takes baby steps with me, preparing me from bed to chair to altar. Finding a pile of floor cushions, I stacked them up and played around with the pillows until I found an arrangement that was comfortable for me to sit. Gazing at my altar from the new perspective of sitting on the floor, I saw and felt the power that had been created in that small spot in my home.

I lit candles and incense, and allowed my body to dictate how to sit: cross-legged, with my palms facing up on my knees. This became my sitting position—no fancy lotus position, but a relaxed open body with a straight spine supported by pillows. This was my new practice: taking the time to sit at my altar each day for about twenty minutes, sometimes less and sometimes more. On some days when I felt called to sit outside under a tree instead, I honored that feeling by carrying my pillow out and sitting wherever nature told me to.

A communication was developing, almost as if my altar had become a living being. At times, it asked for a particular item to be put out into the sunlight or the moonlight. Other times, my altar beckoned objects in the house to be placed upon it to charge them with energy. Frequently, all of my gemstones and crystals ended up on my altar at the same time to be renewed or reprogrammed, and then the knowingness would be placed in me to disperse the gemstones throughout my home. My altar loved to be fed and relished in the burst of energy when flowers, plants, or herbs were set on it.

Over the years, my altar has changed continually, sometimes being so crowded there wasn't room for one more feather. At other times, it wanted to be very simple, with only a feather, a candle, a cup of water, a stick of incense, and a family photo. I love how it ebbs and flows with the unfolding of my personal growth.

Whenever I move to a new home, my altar is what I unpack first. I mark the box it's in very clearly so I can go right to it to see my sacred objects again. It is the very first thing I set up after my bed, and sometimes before! It gets to work immediately, cleansing our new space and filling it with the consciousness we have created together. When I lived in the Hollywood Hills, I was honored and privileged to have *Los Angeles Times Magazine* come out and photograph my altar for a story they were doing about vastu, the East Indian version of feng shui.

But what I love most about having a sacred altar space in my home is what it reminds me of every time I walk by it. I am reminded of the hard work I have done and the healing I have accomplished. I am reminded of how much I have fallen in love with my life. I am reminded of the special time I have each day in the stillness of my mind.

If setting up an altar seems too strange for you or does not interest you, that is fine. My desire to make an altar came naturally to me and is something I wanted to do. If you have a desire to create one, make it your own— it can look however you want it to look. You don't even have to call it an altar; it can just be your special place where you heal your-self.

CREATE AN OUTDOOR SACRED PLACE

You may want to consider making a special, sacred place for yourself outside—especially in a garden, if you have one—so you can fully relax and be with nature. It could be as simple as getting a statue of Mother Mary, Buddha, St. Francis (patron saint of animals), or some other ornamentation that makes you happy. It could be a bench or lounger to relax in under a shade umbrella, or perhaps a hammock or a big pillow to sit upon. You can make your special place very simple or create an entire outdoor room. The idea is to get outside with nature, and having a place that beckons you out the door is helpful. You may even find that you really enjoy this special place and look forward to spending time there.

My special outdoor places always have a make-shift altar that starts out with a favorite stone or crystal. Over time more little things show up, such as feathers and other found objects, incense, and candles. I love to see how it evolves, and unlike my altar inside my home, it doesn't need cleaning.

I don't keep a routine in my special garden place; it remains free of rules and expectations, and exists only for sitting and being with Mother Earth. I feel my garden beckoning to me on days when I have been inside writing and working. It calls to me, asking that I drop everything and have a visit. Most often I comply, because it is always a pleasurable experience, and I am most certainly guaranteed a shift in my energy that day.

There are days when I simply go out and sit, observing the sounds and smells, and watching the birds and bugs go about their business. I find this type of observation to be very satisfying, and it drops me quickly into a nice, relaxed state. My cat may come to sit on my lap or lie on my chest, and have a purr and a snuggle.

Most days, I bring my journal and write in the garden, whether I am writing for work or for pleasure. When I write outside, I feel the grounding energy of the earth surrounding me in a supportive embrace. And on days when I need to write about something particularly emotional, the animal kingdom always brings its energy closer: the neighborhood birds come to watch from a nearby branch, and the squirrels stop their endless chasing to slow down, sit, and watch. The trees feel like they are anchored deep into the earth, my eternal guards holding space for me. This gives me the strength to go deeper and connect with my feelings, because a force greater than myself is holding me.

If you don't have a patio or garden space, you can still create a nature oasis in an apartment! If you have a window, you can have plants. Plants will enliven your space and improve the air quality; and you may find that you enjoy tending to the plants—watering and dusting, and making sure they haven't outgrown their pots. Bring other items into your space from the outdoors, such as a seashell or a sea-glass collection. Rocks, sticks, driftwood, pinecones, herbs, and flowers are all great things to bring indoors. Buy a small table fountain so you can hear the sound of running water. Creating an indoor garden space can be a fun way to bring some creativity into your life while connecting with nature.

Discovering and Experiencing Places of Power

Mother Earth has gifted us with land all over the world that contains powerful energy. Some places are well known, such as Machu Picchu, while others are not, and probably have yet to be discovered. Just as I feel the calling to go out into my special place in the garden, I also receive the pull to visit places that have powerful energy. This could be as simple as visiting the ocean, the desert, or a mountaintop—all of which are readily available to most people.

There are also special places that have been created by aware and conscious people for the sole purpose of healing and bringing people together in community. These can be found at healing and spiritual centers, in their meditation rooms or gardens. I have gone hiking and found small sacred spaces people have created, such as medicine wheels made from rocks. I always receive different information during meditation at these places than I would receive at home. It is almost as if they have called to me so that I may receive a message that wants to be delivered. And for me to hear the message, my energy must be attuned to their particular energy.

I know I must be ready for anything when I make my pilgrimage, so I pack a small backpack with water, snacks, sunscreen, a hat, and my journal. I've learned the hard way that my mind simply will not retain information, and I must write things down in the moment. I have also learned that when I go to public places, even if they are set up for meditation, there will be loud people and interruptions, so earplugs are always in my kit.

I've learned to pay attention to what is annoying me: I allow it to flow through me, acknowledge it, and then set it aside and get to the quiet place within. Never be disappointed when visiting a sacred place if you don't get a big "lightbulb" moment. Maybe next time. Sometimes I do get a big idea or a breakthrough on an issue I have been working on, but on most occasions there is a subtle but important message, or simply a need for a different energy to enter my field.

At one particular Zen location, as I sat and connected with nature, she revealed herself slowly, unfolding her story above my head. Hawks circled, appearing out of nowhere and screeching their message to me with both their voices and their presence. I silently gave thanks for their message and took in the beauty of their visit.

I keep a watchful eye to see who will come to visit: a hummingbird, a butterfly, a lizard. Rather than try to interpret what their message is, I simply acknowledge their visit, taking it all in with my whole being. Until the day I die and return to the earth, I will be connected to my earth mother. I have a relationship with her that is unlike any other. She is my true mother, friend, confidant, healer, supporter, silent partner, and guardian of my path. She has taught me beauty, patience, creativity, and perseverance. She has allowed me to experience her fully and for that I am grateful.

It is my wish that you, too, can have your own profound experiences and meaningful interactions while in nature. We all have our own way to relate with each other and with our environment. What I described to you in this section is based on how I filter life, but you may have a much different experience. I know many people who have a deep relationship with the earth and don't care at all about gemstones, feathers, and the like. These are tools that call to me and that I enjoy using. But remember: this book is all about *you* and your life experience, and as your guide, I am simply sharing my own journey with you to help lead the way.

This is the end of Pillar One and your practice of clearing your mind. After you spend some time practicing and settle into a routine, it will get easier. Everybody will struggle at some point, but that is part of the practice; working through the struggle is part of the action you must take. Remember that at the beginning of the book, I talked about these processes being free and readily available to everybody, and advised not to discount them because they appear simple. Simple doesn't mean easy, and free doesn't mean worthless.

Many people ask me how they will know when their mind is clear. You will know. You will feel yourself slip into a relaxed state, and a supreme sense of peace will envelop you. When you are first practicing, you may "pop out" of this state once you realize you are in it. This is natural— don't feel like you are doing anything wrong. What is important is that you are *doing* it. You are taking action—doing real work—and it will bring results.

3

Pillar Two:
Nurture Your Spirit

The phrase *mind, body, spirit* has really come into our everyday vocabulary over the last ten years. The word *Spirit* can be confusing to people—is it God? In terms of my work, Spirit means your soul and your connection to a greater source, which I call the Universe.

Your soul is not a body part; it is the true essence of who you are at a core level. For example, when you feel a calling to do something great in the world, that is your soul calling. When you are having a conversation with somebody and you get goose bumps or your hair stands on end, that is your soul listening. Your soul, not your mind or body, is the part of you that has come to earth to grow and learn. The soul often gets neglected because it is not seen, but it is the soul that calls out to you to turn your life around. When you are in your meditative state and when you are communing with nature, it is your soul that presents itself to you, making itself known.

Many people are completely out of touch with their soul selves, either because they don't know they have one or they are self-medicating to keep it hidden. The work you will do with Pillar Two will help you get more in touch with your soul, opening doorways to it that have been shut for a long time. Through a process of daily writing, you will start to awaken what has been dormant. I will teach you what to write and the process of starting a daily journaling practice. You will also be asked to write about topics that are unique to you and your own situation.

In this pillar, I will also talk about fear, self-sabotage, and forgiveness: all very powerful challenges and worth all of the time you put into exploring them. As you proceed through each section, do so at your own pace; if you start to feel overwhelmed, you can pull back a little. Take a pause and stay where you are, working with the program so you have time to be with your feelings. One effective and easy yoga pose I often use to help me when I feel overwhelmed is called "child's pose." You get into the pose by sitting on your knees and then bringing your forehead to the floor. Your arms can be next to your sides or stretched out in front. The act of bringing your forehead to the floor is very grounding to your body, connecting you with the earth. Breathe softly, and stay in the pose for as long as you like.

There is no time limit or constraint when attending to your healing. Each of us has our own unique pace, our own flow through the process. It is always important to be gentle with yourself and honor feelings that come up during your practice.

I also write about opening your creative center. This is very important, because when that part of yourself is shut down, fear and depression can take up residence. Once you learn to open yourself to being a creative person, you will wonder why you didn't go for it earlier in your life. *Creativity* can mean many things, and it doesn't matter what you do but how you do it—with your creative consciousness. I will ask you to take a journey to find your creative self, and I guarantee you it will be fun and exciting. Creativity can be done alone or with a group; there are absolutely no restrictions when it comes to being creative!

At the end of this chapter, I will introduce the idea of being of service to others. When we need to *get out of our own way,* being of service to others provides a quick means to doing this. Sending out the "I'm available" signal to be of assistance to somebody is truly selfless and is a wonderful balance to all of the hard emotional work you will be doing. By the time you reach the end of the book, you will have a balanced healing foundation in place that will serve your mind, body, and soul for the rest of your life.

Step 1: Write as if Your Life Depended on It (Five to Seven Days a Week)

I consider journaling and meditation two of the most important tools in my healing toolbox. Both of these practices are powerful agents of change. And when you use them in tandem, there is nothing you cannot accomplish. You will also appreciate that both of these practices are absolutely free and available to each and every person on the planet.

Journaling can take many forms, and it is possible to have multiple journals going at the same time if that interests you. Some examples include an art journal, a manifestation and goal-setting journal, a new-ideas journal, and a journal dedicated to writing just about your children or your family. For the purposes of healing, I suggest a journal for your feelings and intro-spection.

People ask me all the time, "Why do I need to journal? Why can't I just think the thoughts rather than write them down?" There are many answers to this question, and the first is that taking the time to sit and gather your pen and journal is an *action*—a preparation and declaration that you are ready for change. When you are thinking thoughts in the shower, you are busy washing yourself and not fully focused on the thoughts. The act of sitting to write is a ritual, and there is an energy behind it that is created when you treat it as such.

Another reason for journaling your thoughts rather than just thinking them is that something happens when pen meets paper. When I took my young son to be blessed by Amma, the hugging saint, a gentleman gave a talk beforehand. He told us that if we handed anything to Amma, we should do so with our right hand, because there is a nerve that connects the right hand to the brain. (As I am writing this, I can feel an energy flow from my brain to my fingers. I do a lot of my book writing in longhand!) Writing is ultimately a brain connection we can do with either the left or the right hand—the point is taking the action to make that connection.

We usually cannot write as fast as we can think our thoughts, so by sitting with pen and paper, we slow down, drop fully into the task at hand, and create energy. When we simply think a thought, we have the tendency to change the subject if we are at all uncomfortable, and that is usually where the juicy tidbits are hiding. Thinking about our issues allows us to cleverly gloss over what we don't want to address, but we can't get away with that behavior while writing. Journaling slows the process, allowing you to peel back a layer to look at difficult issues in safety.

The writing process brings new things to the surface. Allow me a train metaphor, if you will. The mind is used to being stuck on a certain track, and the writing process takes you off that track and onto a new one. On the new track, you will find the answers that you need in order to get to the station—there really is no other practice that can do this for you. Don't be surprised if you really end up loving to journal every day and soon look forward to it.

Now that you have slowed your mind by writing with a pen, new thoughts are allowed to emerge as if they have been given permission to come forth. The racing of the mind has calmed, and a rhythm is formed as your pen glides across the page. When the mind has been slowed, thoughts aren't competing to be blurted out and will wait their turn to be fully realized. Knowing this allows a thought to reach its full potential, and many layers begin to unfold before you.

When journaling, it is of utmost importance that you do not judge what comes forth. The critical mind will shut down your thought process quicker than anything else. Allow your words to flow; don't worry about sentence structure, grammar, or spelling errors. Write like nobody is reading! Try not to worry if it is good or worthy. You are exploring your thoughts and feelings, and you are entitled to them. Do not let the fear of somebody else reading your work stop you from writing from the deepest part of yourself. If this is a concern for you, I suggest you leave the first page blank, and on the second page, write "Personal writing of (your name); please do not read." If necessary, you can find a place to hide your journal. Mostly, however, this fear stems from your brain and is a way to stop you from journaling. We are brilliant at stopping emotional healing in its tracks—"Self-Sabotage 101."

I have stacks of journals that I have filled over the thirty years I have been journaling. They are so precious to me that I keep them in a fireproof safe, and they would be one of the first things I would save if I needed to leave my house quickly. I rarely go back and read from them, but when I do, they are a storehouse of valuable information. On days when I feel trapped and depressed that I have not made progress with a certain issue, I can refer to my journal from years gone by and read about the progression of a certain problem. I *always* find that I have made great progress and that the situation has changed significantly. Without the access to my writing, I would not have the paper trail of my journey to reference. You don't need to save your journals if you don't want to; some people actually prefer to burn them as ritual—this part doesn't matter. What matters is that you write.

Journaling, for me, is one of my favorite parts of the day. I live in California, so most days are sunny enough to take my pen and journal outside to write in my special place. Surprisingly, journaling became something that I needed to learn: not the writing part but the ritual of taking the time each day to journal. Often I would sit and be distracted by nature, or drift off to sleep, or stare at a blank page. I came to realize that these were all small forms of self-sabotage; I never imagined that the practice of journaling would be just that—a practice. I berated myself for not being able to do the simplest of actions—to sit and write in a notebook. The solution to this is: be gentle with yourself! It does no good beating yourself up. Just take a breath, notice the behavior, and make a correction.

It may surprise you that I don't journal in fancy leather journals. I go to the drugstore and buy 99-cent spiral-bound notebooks and decorate them myself. This allows me to have some time for creativity, and it starts the symbiosis with my energy being infused into the new journal. It is like I'm blessing it while decorating the cover, as I know that we have important work to do together. My relationship with my journal is personal, intimate, intense, and sacred.

My dirty secret is that when I first started to journal, I didn't think my writing would be worth putting in a nice leather journal; I thought a nice journal was too good for me. This, too, became part of the process as feelings of unworthiness showed up for me just in time to write about them. I would advise selecting a journal that you will use, whether you buy a cheap one, make your own, or get a fancy one. Also, your journals don't need to match, and once you fill one up, the next one doesn't have to be the same type.

If you are new to journaling, a beautiful act you can perform is to write a dedication to yourself on the very first page. Write whatever comes to you, and it will be perfect. Try not to come up with the perfect paragraph or poem, just write a promise to yourself and a dedication to the journaling practice you are about to undertake. Here is a dedication I wrote years ago in a journal (completely unedited stream of consciousness):

> I promise to take the time each day to connect with myself, to allow for my Soul to shine and express itself. I'm worth the time for creative expression and release of mental clutter to uncover the good stuff waiting to be heard. My Soul's desire waits to be witnessed and to be guardian of my life. I am open to change and welcome spirit to work with me and through me as I write. I promise not to judge what comes forth from the layers as they gently show what lies beneath. I know I am protected and strong and I honor all parts of myself as they are revealed.

WHAT DO I WRITE ABOUT?

Another question I'm often asked is, "What do I write about?" The easy answer is to write, without judgment, about whatever wants to come out. This journal is for your emotional happiness, so you will more than likely be writing about your feelings. But I also believe in journaling with intention—with a desired result in mind—and this would be the harder answer to the question of what to write about.

The result of your daily journaling is the peeling back of layers to get to the root of your issue(s). It is the road to self-discovery in a safe and effective process. If you find yourself very wound up, I suggest keeping a separate journal or loose-leaf pages and just writing from the top of your head. What I mean by that is to write down all the clutter in your head: perhaps the to-do lists first, followed by all the thoughts that are sitting on top, blocking you. Once you get all of the clutter out, your brain will naturally slow down, and you will feel the shift of settling into your journaling with intention.

After you are settled, write at the top of the page, "Please reveal to me what I need to know. Show me the way." If you want to begin the sentence with "God," another divine deity, or your higher self, feel free—make it your own. It is important, however, that you write the sentence, because this sets the stage; you are now intending to dig deep, explore, and examine what is holding you back. Remember: don't hold back no matter what comes out.

Please do not be hard on yourself if nothing wants to come forth immediately. This is not at all uncommon at first; it is simply another fear of not wanting to see what is hidden. In this case, take the opportunity to look at the fear and make your journaling time about that.

I consider journaling a very important tool that enables me to reach depths I cannot reach through meditation or thought. As I noted earlier, when we are all on our metaphorical train, living our lives, we tend to stay on the same track. What I love about journaling is that it lovingly bumps us off the track so we can notice something new. Use journaling to address all of your problems and discover your own solutions. You could think of yourself as being your own best oracle—your journal knows all the answers! If you are working on a specific problem, let the journaling process aid you. Start by writing the question or problem at the top of the page, and go from there.

Allow yourself a few weeks to settle into the process. Let go. Remember: Help is given to those who ask. If you ask the Universe for assistance, the Universe will answer the call. You will not be left on your own, but it *is* up to you to recognize the help when it arrives. The help may not come in the form you had imagined or expected, but it will come. Keep your eyes open, do your practice, use all of your senses so that you will notice when your help arrives. If you ever read the Harry Potter books or saw the movies, you will remember this line: "Help will

always be given at Hogwarts to those who ask."
Ditto with Spirit!

Before I close out this journaling section,
I want to address men directly: If you think
journaling is for the ladies, I believe you feel this
way because society has taught you that feelings
are for women. This couldn't be further from the
truth, and I encourage you to journal about *your*
feelings. If you are feeling embarrassed for some
reason, you don't need to tell anybody you are
doing it. Don't let these feelings interfere with
a process that will be enormously beneficial to
your life and well-being.

HEALING YOUR FEAR

**People's two biggest fears are not getting what
they want and losing what they have.** Sit with
that for a moment and see how true it is for you.
Maybe you have always wanted a particular
home or job or relationship, and once you have
it, you spend your time worrying about losing it!
When you are in fear, you are saying that you are
not good enough—not worthy. What you want
to do is shift into a place of peace and balance,
and when you find that beautiful sweet spot,
you won't care about either of those fears or any
others.

But getting to the root of fear requires

some work on your part. It requires dedicated journaling without an expectation of how long the process will take. The process is different for everybody; there is no right or wrong amount of time, because you are uniquely you. I was the world's biggest scaredy cat, and fear is a huge part of my recovery. I'm scared of so many things: the dark, crowds, tiny places, big places, anything unknown, flying, spiders (not flying spiders!), dying before I raise my child, car crashes, drowning, crocodiles and sharks, loud noises, the dentist, computer programing, somehow ending up in jail, heights, and more. Uncovering the layers of fear and looking at them can be really uncomfortable, making you squirm. I get it. But for right now, we are just going to take a peek, and you will be safe.

Here are some points I would like you to write about.

1. Make a list of the fears in your life.
2. Write about each of them in depth, including the benefits you get from having each fear.
3. How long have you had these fears? At what age did each fear begin?
4. What part of your body is reacting? Where do you feel it—in your chest, your gut? Breathe into that space and be with it; really feel it.

5. How does fear keep you from making choices in your life?
6. Write one to three ways you can take action against each fear.

Here is a journal excerpt from a time when fear came up for me and I was blocked. (It has been edited to maintain privacy.) In this particular case, I was having a conversation with Spirit:

Please reveal to me where my fear is coming from.
I am feeling fearful right now, and I just don't want to deal with it. I wish it would just go away.

Where in your body do you feel the fear?
My chest feels tight, and it is hard to catch my breath.
(Breathing.)

And what is this fear telling you?
That it is not safe to do something.

And what is the worst thing that would happen if you did this thing?
I could be made a fool of, I would be embarrassed, and people will think I'm dumb and not good enough.

What part of you would feel embarrassed?
The part of me that says, "I'm not good enough"—the part of me that my dad ridiculed all the time.

Is any of what he said true?
No.

Do you realize that you are denying yourself every time you reject yourself? In essence, you are calling Spirit a liar, because you are perfect the way you are in every moment.
(Sigh. Tears.)

SELF-SABOTAGE: WHY DO WE DO IT?

I am constantly amazed by how brilliant we human beings are when it comes to sabotaging our lives. We are so sneaky at it that most of the time we don't even realize we are doing it. I, too, was a master saboteur, queen of the excuse, CEO of control, and gold-medal winner for creativity in the category of procrastination. And self-sabotage comes in so many sneaky forms. See if any of these sound familiar to you: overcommitting your time, being indecisive and ambivalent, creating "busyness," always coming up with excuses, having a stronghold of what you will and will not do, and addiction. When we think of addiction, mostly alcohol and drugs come to mind, and possibly food. But there are many other ways we throw a blanket over ourselves, as I wrote earlier. Anything that gets out of balance can become an addiction.

With any behavior, we need to look at the motivation behind the behavior, or as I like to say, "What or who is driving that bus?" Humans only continue behaviors if those behaviors are working for them—if they are getting something out of that behavior or substance use that they like or derive pleasure from. We all sabotage ourselves to some degree; once you start to identify the self-sabotaging actions you take in *your* life, you can begin to heal the hurt underneath. And because we are experts in the art of self-sabotage, it is important to know that once you locate your patterns, you may be so brilliant that you pull a bait and switch on yourself, hiding your self-sabotage elsewhere. Kindly let your body know that you are aware of your own tricks!

So why do we sabotage ourselves so much?

The answer is big. **When we self-sabotage, we don't have to show up for our life.** Sit with that for a while and really take it in. Self-sabotage is fear based, and most of us go through life with our fear leading the way—but we don't even know it. We may be very good at seeing it in other people, but we rarely see it in ourselves. We have to examine it more closely, peeling back the layers to see what is at the core. I don't know of anyone who doesn't have fear in their lives. We are humans on a journey, and if we didn't have issues, we probably wouldn't be incarnated in a body! I say that to lessen any feelings of failure you may be feeling now. Trust me when I tell you there is nothing wrong with you; you are just going to shift things around a bit so you can lead the life you really want.

Think of all the ways you have created blocks of fear to keep you from reaching your goals. Know that habitual behaviors become like friends or entities that live within us. When you start to identify your own patterns, some extra fear and panic may come up. This is because you have lived with the behavior for a long time, and it has been good to you. It has protected and taken care of you the way you needed it to, and you are used to it; it is a part of you.

When I started to heal my self-sabotaging behaviors, I felt like I was in mourning and was actually sad. The grief came from the deepest aspect of me, which recognized that I was only doing what I had to do in order to stay alive in the world. This was a crucial time, and I knew that tending to my grief with gentleness and kindness was the only way I could ease out of it. Powering through it was not an option, and that would be disrespectful of the process. In fact, it would be yet another form of self-sabotaging by skimming only the surface and not fully feeling the process.

You can do a writing exercise in your journal to address this sadness just like you did for the work on fear. Spend as much time as you need; it will probably take more than one sitting. In fact, over time more layers will be revealed. This is the beautiful thing about the writing process: as you heal and become more comfortable with your feelings, more will show up to be cleared. Never edit yourself. Always write down what comes up, even if it makes you feel embarrassed or surprised.

Here are some things to write about and examine:

1. Write a list of ways that you sabotage your life.
2. For each behavior, write the reasons you self-sabotage in that way: what is the root of that behavior?
3. Write one or more different choices you can make for each behavior.
4. From this point forward, notice throughout your day when you self-sabotage. Make a mental note and try to shift out of it. Awareness is key to shifting, so begin to be aware of these behaviors.

Remember that shifting behavior rarely happens overnight, so be gentle with yourself while you are going through these processes. There is never a need to rush, and your journey through healing will be unique to you.

Step 2: Write a Letter

You can also use your journal for another powerful process: letter writing. In this step, you want to locate the emotional pain that is held in your body. This will be different for everybody, so again, try not to judge what comes up. You may want to "name" the fear, or you may find that you want to write to a child aspect of yourself or to an internal organ, such as your heart or liver. I know that might sound strange, but our bodies hold on to everything we have ever experienced in our life unless we let it go. More often than not, you will be targeting a fragmented part of yourself that wants to be heard and will not stand down until it is heard fully.

This may take days of journaling and processing, or even longer. When I worked the process on myself, I found several fractured aspects of my inner child from various ages, so I had a lot of writing to do. The most scared and sad part of me was a young girl who needed a lot of attention. When I switched into survival mode as a child, a part of me was left behind, unattended to. I knew that if I started to communicate with her, I absolutely could not, under any circumstances, abandon her again.

I wrote to her, I sat quietly with her, and I did things that I thought she would enjoy, such as feeding ducks at the pond. I imagined that she was with me all the time; it was almost like bringing a toddler around during the day. When I drove the car, I pictured her sitting next to me. This child in me really wanted to be heard and seen, and I even bought her a fairy coloring book and some colored pencils. It doesn't matter how you approach this; it will be different for everybody. What mattered was that I was giving that part of myself the attention she needed so I could go on to heal her hurt feelings. Later, when I began writing to the older eight-year-old me and the teenager me, I found that those ages didn't need so much mothering and attention; the letter writing was less dramatic.

You can start this exercise with a meditation session, getting quiet, calm, and clearheaded. Write on the top of the page: "Please show me where my pain resides." Don't worry if you are left staring at a blank page; the pain may not be ready to surface yet, and that is okay. Keep trying the exercise each day until something shows up. Write down whatever comes to you, even if it seems silly and even if you think you are making it up. Then you can leave your writing as is, in journal form, or you can go on to write it to yourself in a letter format.

When you locate and uncover where the pain resides, you must give it what it needs: love, attention, and trust. By writing down what comes to you, you are demonstrating to the part of you that is wounded that it can trust you. Where there is trust, there is flow. You will know when you have made an authentic connection with the part of you that needs healing, as it will not ask for sugar or drugs, or to obsessively clean the house; it will simply want to be heard. As humans, we all want to have our pain and suffering witnessed.

As we become more and more disassociated from each other in American society, the need to be heard becomes greater. This is why blogging and social media have become so popular— everybody gets to be heard. But sadly, we do not receive human-to-human, eye-to-eye contact or a hug from our computers, and we are left feeling almost as empty despite sharing our feelings with the world.

Healing fear does not come overnight. Locating the source of the fear is monumental—a very important step that you should not skip or rush. It creates the necessary change to set up the healing shift in your life.

A LETTER OF FORGIVING YOURSELF

I am a big believer in the power of forgiveness. Unfortunately, it is a process that most people don't want to look at or attempt, because they "just don't want to go there." I understand. There are often so many emotions and feelings around the topic of forgiveness. At some point, though, you must look at it and go through the process. When you come out on the other side, you will wonder why you didn't do it earlier. For now, I want to plant the seed in you and give a nudge; when you feel ready, it would be wonderful if you could work on forgiveness. Until then, I will walk with you gingerly, not because I need to but because I respect your feelings.

It is important to note that most often, when we hear the word *forgiveness,* we think about forgiving somebody else. But I want to offer the idea that you may also need to forgive yourself. We are all so hard on ourselves; you, too, may have pushed down feelings of guilt, unworthiness, and other strong emotions, hiding them away so you can pretend they aren't there. You are human and therefore fallible; you are on your journey and that includes what you might call mistakes, or what I call learning experiences. Forgive yourself for everything—all of the negative self-talk, being mean to the kid next to you in third grade, saying horrible things to your partner or your children, having bad thoughts, lying, cheating, or stealing. Forgive yourself for all of it because you are worth it, and it does no good walking around with a heavy burden tucked away, festering until it can hide no more.

Write a letter to yourself, forgive yourself, and set yourself free. Write in your journal without editing your feelings around this topic. Write about what you want to forgive yourself for and make a promise that from now on, you will try to be kinder to yourself. As always, don't judge what comes out, and write from your heart, not your head. It is up to you how often you want to write this letter of forgiveness—it may be every day for a month or once a week for a year. Buy yourself some flowers and know you are doing something you have been waiting for.

A LETTER OF FORGIVING ANOTHER

We also like to hang on to our anger and resentment of others so we don't have to go through the process of forgiveness. We refuse to let go because we think that forgiving them is somehow condoning their behavior or letting them off the hook. Our ego tells us to hold on to this illusion so it can be protected—so we don't have to do the real work—and we keep on suffering. When we set ourselves free of the burden of this old story, our ego no longer has that job to do, and our mind wonders, *What now?* But hanging on to these powerful feelings keeps us small and unable to live our life to the fullest. I ask you to look at the price you pay for holding on to your anger and resentment. Are you willing to risk your health to hold steadfast in your stubbornness? Allow yourself to let go of the pain.

Forgiveness is a process and rarely an overnight fix. If you are ready to forgive, it may come quickly, but it may take some time. I've had forgiveness happen within the same day or take several months, and I know a person who took years to unravel the layers. Forgiveness is for *you,* not the person you are forgiving. This person doesn't even need to know you are doing the work; you don't need to forgive face to face (unless you want to). This is about you and for you, and you can do it in the privacy of your journal.

Make a list of people you want to forgive, and start writing a letter to each of these people. How did they make you feel in the past, and how do you feel about them now? The letter is for you to work on in your journal and doesn't need to be mailed. You will know the work is done when you are no longer triggered by these people— when you can allow the old feelings to wash away and send them along with feelings of peace.

At the top of my own list of people I wanted to

forgive was my father, who died at age sixty-nine when I was twenty-nine years old. By writing and examining my feelings about my dad, I came to the important realization that I no longer blamed him for his abuse. We are all responsible for our own lives, and our own thoughts and actions. When I learned more about my parents' own childhoods and how they suffered, everything began to make sense to me. It doesn't make my dad's actions okay, but it helps with healing and forgiveness. Now, as I raise my own child, I commit each and every day to doing things differently—to breaking the family cycle and creating something new. There comes a time when, as adults, we must stop blaming and take the initiative to find peace and acceptance with our trauma. We must patiently, gently, and slowly create a new, healthy reality through the process of forgiveness.

A final note: Imagine that you are high above the earth, looking down. Billions of people are living out and trying to navigate their lives—all of them on their own journeys. For some, it may be their first life on earth, and others may have had many lives. Each time we come back into a body, we have an agenda, and most of that agenda has to do with other people and our relationship to them. You have agreements set up ahead of time about how things are going to play out, and people will come into your life to shake things up for you, either by acting as a mirror or by helping you to have an experience so you have the opportunity to work through that experience. This is where growth resides; it is the "good stuff," although we don't perceive it as such. Know that your life has meaning and purpose, and if you have somebody to forgive, do the work. The rewards are so worth it.

Step 3: Take Time to Create
(Twice a Week, Minimum)

After the emotional heaviness of this chapter, this next step will lighten things up. Many of us were told at some point in our life that we couldn't sing, draw, paint, or write well enough—and it stuck with us. Maybe you put this label on yourself, adding to the shame you carry. But we human beings are meant to create! At the highest level, we create how we live our lives each day, and within that day, we can choose to have creative time to make something tangible.

Creativity is a powerhouse force within all of us that is just waiting to be tapped. When we are in a creative mode, an energy flow connects mind, body, and soul in a beautiful rhythm. When I write this, the feeling I get is almost one of finding a golden key and putting it into a locked treasure box to reveal the hidden treasure within all of us. Whether you are making sand castles at the beach, sitting at a potter's wheel, decorating a room, writing poetry, painting, knitting, or building a house, you have the potential to be creative. Even if you don't have traditional art tools, you can create art with sticks, rocks, and dirt; in fact, children do this naturally. Mud pies, sand smoothies, and finger painting were some of our earliest art forms, and we did them without editing, without judgment, and with pure joy.

What I love about creativity is that it is a beautiful respite from doing hard emotional work. It can be like a mini vacation for your soul. Some people, however, use their art as part of their healing process, and this work produces deeply emotional art that is palpable upon viewing. Making art can be a meditation in action as the paint touches down on the canvas or the knitting needles begin to clack. Allow yourself to explore your creative side.

I was born into a creative family, including a famous printmaker. People in my family write, paint, draw, quilt, carve, and sculpt. I, on the other hand, found at an early age that I was not good at those things. I did have an ear for music and I was a dancer, but what I really wanted to do was paint or draw as well as my family members. What actually happened is that I labeled myself as a "bad artist" and shut myself down. But I'm not the only wounded artist—you may be one as well. We are everywhere.

Even though my family was creative, creativity was not something to base a serious career on. My parents made it clear to me that I would not be able to make money in a creative industry. In high school my father was mad at me because he demanded that I become an engineer or an accountant, but I hated math. As a project, he made me go through the help-wanted classified ads in the newspaper and pick out jobs that interested me. Nothing appealed to me in those ads. There was nothing creative and certainly nothing relating to the film industry, which very much interested me. This made my father angry. He decided that I should be a secretary, and if I was to be a secretary, I needed to be a very good typist. He made me type after school for a couple of hours each day, and I had to deliver the typed papers to him at the dinner table. My creativity was crushed.

Never allow somebody to crush your dreams. It may take some time for your dreams to come true, but hold on to them dearly. Your creative expression is as natural to you as how you walk, how you speak, and how you put yourself out into the world. You were born a creative being, and opening your creative center is a vital tool to your expression of yourself in the world.

When I began to unlock my creativity, I found

the vitality and excitement in my life that had long been missing. I noticed books, magazines, and ads for various creative ventures, and after seeing enough of these signs, I realized I needed to reawaken my creativity in a way that made sense to me. I needed to find a creative outlet that made me happy and perhaps something that I could be good at. I picked up knitting needles and formed a knitting group that met at my house each Sunday. I started an art journal, took riding lessons, visited museums, sewed projects for my house, and colored in books. There was no way I could ignore all of the signs the Universe was sending me: I needed to get creative and find something that resonated with me. Not everything worked out; I'm not a great knitter, and my art journal doesn't look like a work of art. But I excelled in other things and felt great joy and a wonderful sense of accomplishment.

I decided that each day I would create something using my imagination. My only stipulation was that I could not judge what I made—no inner voice could tell me it wasn't good enough or that it should be immediately relegated to the trash. This was art for me, and realizing that I didn't need to show anybody my work allowed me the freedom to just create. This can be an important aspect of your creativity; it is okay to keep it to yourself if you want to. After all, you aren't sending out invitations to an art show featuring your work—not quite yet anyway!

Trying a variety of creative outlets worked so well for me that at one point, I turned a creative idea into a hobby, and the hobby turned into a business. After a short while, my small aromatherapy company (candles, essential oils, and the like) turned into a $500,000-a-year company without even giving it my fullest effort. I tell you this because you never know where creativity will lead you! Allow it to guide you and to flow, and you will be fully rewarded.

Many times when I am feeling tired or am in between projects, I switch on the TV to watch a movie. I often notice there is something hanging around that I'm trying to avoid, and watching a movie is easier than facing my issue. This is a different feeling than being sick or tired—it is an avoidance behavior. Now that I recognize the pattern, I am able to catch myself when I am about to switch on the TV. I ask myself, *Is there something creative I can do instead?* Most of the time, the answer is yes, and I use my time to enjoy some fun exploration with colored pencils, garden art, sewing, collaging, or weaving. At the end of this effort, I have accomplished something, created something— even made something from nothing—and I feel good.

I wrote earlier that some people use the creative process to work through issues, and art therapy is a wonderful tool. As with journaling, you can use your hands, which are connected to your brain, to make art and access emotions. Rather than writing words on paper, you are making a unique 3-D expression of who you are. This is the beauty of creativity: if I were to put the exact same supplies in front of two people, they would make completely different projects.

Just as everybody has a unique handwriting style, you have your own creative voice—nobody will create in the same way that you do. When you think of it in these terms, you almost owe it to yourself to see what you can bring forth into the world. And making art and being creative don't have to be done publicly; you don't need to have an art show or sell your work. What is important is that you do it, explore it, and enjoy it.

If you aren't quite ready to embrace your creativity, a great leaping-off point is to keep a creativity journal. Here you can write down inspiration or ideas, and perhaps even doodle a bit. Write about all the things you want to try and make lists of art supplies, or keep track of research on art classes. If you choose to, try making art out of the journal itself by painting or collaging the cover. You may even find that art journaling is interesting to you. The sky is the limit, so experiment and make it yours.

Step 4: How May I Be
of Service Today?

We are all so blessed to be alive, though we may not always feel that way. To offer in kind—to be of service to humanity—is a beautiful and humbling act. You will notice immediate change when you begin your morning with the simple words, "How may I be of service today?" You may address your question to Spirit, God, the Universe, Mother Mary—it doesn't matter; it will be heard. It is then up to you to keep your eyes and ears and other senses open and available to pick up on the message of when you are needed and what your task shall be.

This is different from volunteer work, which is also important. Volunteer work usually means going to the same place in an organized way on certain days. Asking how to be of service is a way Spirit can use you as a human angel whenever there is a need. It is like volunteering to be an earth angel each day, and you will be used in kind whenever you ask.

I really can think of nothing sweeter than to be asked for my human vessel to be of assistance to the Spirit realm. To warm your heart further, remember times when you, too, have been the recipient of help at some point in your life. I recognize it now: a stranger interacts with me on a day when I'm feeling depleted or really working hard on overcoming an issue. When the kindness is being delivered to me, I take it in fully and allow them their task, and thank them for their service. Imagine if each person on earth did this seemingly small task every day: what changes would occur on our planet!

I will admit that at first I was hesitant to start this practice, because I thought it meant I would have to make large contributions each day and I didn't feel like I had the strength for that. What I found instead was sweetness, simplicity, ease, and grace. Here are some examples of how I am in service daily: smiling at somebody I normally wouldn't make the effort to smile at; allowing somebody to go in front of me at the grocery store checkout line, even if I'm in a hurry; passing by a closer parking space because I "know" the person behind me needs it more. These sound like basic acts of kindness (and they are), but they are different in the way they are presented to me: they feel like a strong knowing—an intuition—that I need to do these things, and I can feel the energy shift when I complete them.

It is one thing to perform acts of kindness as a courtesy to our fellow humans, but to go out into your day declaring that you are available to be of service changes the playing field entirely. And you know, most of the time these acts of service are also for your own benefit too, as you'll always be left with a lighter heart and happier spirit.

Here is an example of an experience I had where I was used by Spirit to be in the right place at the right time: I was in my car on a rainy California day and had the intuitive thought before I left the house to put on some warmer clothes and wear my wool boots. When I was almost to my destination, I began to feel my car surge forward as if a giant hand was on top of it, urging me along. It was such a strange sensation that I checked all of my dashboard instruments to see if there was a mechanical reason for this feeling of extra forward momentum.

Soon I came to a busy intersection where I needed to make a right turn, but because of the downpour, the turn lane was flooded. I hesitated, unsure about what to do. I needed to pick a lane, and I chose to drive into the deep puddle, hoping it would be safe. I was the first in line at the light when I saw a collision take place in the intersection in front of me, with one of the cars sliding directly at me. I braced for impact and my car was hit. I thought for sure it would be totaled.

When I stepped out of my car into the deep water, I realized why I had had the intuitive thought to wear my wool boots and warm clothes. I went around to the front of my car, bracing myself to see the front end crushed, and I was shocked to see that the only damage was that my license plate had come off and landed somewhere in the puddle. So I then sprang into action to help the injured in the other cars, and I stayed to lend assistance until the ambulance arrived. There was confusion and there were broken bones. One of the drivers asked me to wade through the water to retrieve her purse; I also called her mom. Then I helped hold on to the gentleman in the other car.

I am very good in emergency situations, and I realized I was put in that scene to lend assistance and bring much-needed calming energy. Although my car and I were miraculously uninjured, I was scared to ask the morning service question the next day, as I didn't want to participate in anything like that again. Eventually I set up a guideline: I did not wish to be put in traumatic situations anymore. And I haven't been since.

Another example of being of service is an incident that happened on a sunny day after a walk on the beach with my family. We were heading home when I saw an elderly man riding his bike across the street. He hit the curb with his front wheel and went flying onto the sidewalk. I quickly yelled to my husband to pull over, then I leapt out of the car and ran to help the man. I stayed with him until he was able to stand and we could be sure nothing was broken. He refused a ride home and went on his way, grateful for the assistance. What is interesting about this story is that I had again been put in the right place at the right time: prior to us getting on the road, there had been several delays in getting into the car and out of our parking spot—delays that put me where I needed to be to witness the accident and lend a hand.

I think of this simple daily question and action as coming full circle with the energy of the Universe. It's a powerful way to keep energy flowing, propelling wellness forward and around to the benefit of many.

Optional Step

SEND LOVE AHEAD TO YOUR DAY

Every day, when your eyes first open to the morning light, you have an opportunity to set the tone for your day. Each and every day is a new beginning ripe with the opportunity to live it in the way you desire. Yet so many of us begin the day by opening our eyes and immediately thinking about our to-do list. We engage in our morning rush, taking care of our spouse, children, and pets with little regard to how we are setting up our own day.

Somewhere along the way, during my years of trying to become an enlightened human, I came across a beautiful gesture: sending love ahead to your day. I remember being so touched by both the beauty and the simplicity of the ritual that I immediately put it into practice, falling in love with this blessing *to* me *from* me. It has become a practice that I look forward to in the morning, and knowing that I am giving myself such a thoughtful gift makes waking up so much more pleasurable.

We all see, feel, and hear differently when working on a subtle level—the spiritual playing field. When I send love ahead to my day, I see it in my mind's eye as light streaming from my body and traveling through my day, blessing my every moment until I reach the same time again the next morning. I feel like I am sending myself grace and beauty throughout my day, and I need only stop and "catch" it. This technique has saved me on countless occasions when I have become flustered, angry, or overwhelmed by life. I pause and remember the love I sent myself that very morning, taking it all in, breathing it in, receiving the love and the grace that I had thoughtfully prepared earlier. Quite simply, it is a beautiful practice for which I will always be grateful.

Sending love ahead to my day became particularly important to me when I began to have panic attacks on the freeways of Los Angeles. One particular day, when I was on the freeway with the top down on my convertible, exposed to the elements, heat, and exhaust, I became boxed in by four semitrailers, with no escape. The familiar feelings of anxiety started to grow quickly within me: I was short of breath, I could feel my entire body beginning to sweat, and my mind started racing. I was consumed by a full-fledged panic attack within ten seconds. My mind filled with options, including jumping out of the car and running to the side of the road. I needed to escape—to get out of the feeling of being trapped.

The fight-or-flight response was fully engaged, and somewhere deep inside, I pleaded with myself to not do anything rash. But even knowing that I was not going to die in that moment was not enough to calm me down. There was no getting out of the situation, so I needed to deal with it and do what I could while trapped in my car. I took a sip of water and then grabbed a tight hold on the heart-shaped rose-quartz crystal I keep in my car for this very type of emergency. I grasped and reached fully for the love I had sent to myself that morning, allowing it to wash over me and consume me so there would be no room for panic. The love and light calmed me down enough that I was able to get my husband on speakerphone to just be on the line with me, so I wouldn't feel alone, until I drove into the safety of my driveway.

This is an extreme example of how I have used the love I send myself every morning. On most occasions, I stop to feel the love when I'm paying bills, or when I need strength to deal with my young son, or when I'm standing in a slow line at the grocery store. I believe you will really enjoy incorporating this lovely gesture into your own life.

4

Pillar Three:
Strengthen Your Body

Our bodies work hard for us, taking the physical abuse of poor eating habits and toxins from various sources. They take emotional abuse when we tell ourselves we are not good enough or we don't like what we see in the mirror. In truth there is only so much abuse our bodies will take before disease, premature aging, weight gain, and other maladies appear. In order to have a complete package of a healthy mind, body, and spirit, we must pay attention to the physical body and its needs.

When I speak of strengthening your body, I am not talking about lifting weights and creating muscle; I am referring to building your body from the inside out. This is a gradual process, which includes eating correctly, taking supplements, and cutting out sugar. Think of your body as a seed: how can the seed grow if it isn't provided nutrient-rich soil, water, and sun? Depending on your age, it can take a while to complete the process of building a strong body. As you eliminate what isn't good for you, such as sugar, junk food, fast food, cigarettes, and too much alcohol, your body will take notice and begin to heal.

By adding in what is good for you, such as wholesome, organic food and supplements, you will be on your path to creating a stronger body. Including healing modalities like massage, acupuncture, chiropractic care, and more can greatly enhance your well-being, and I would highly recommend you seek out holistic practitioners in these areas.

Finding a good team of people to help me through my healing process was crucial. Currently on my team, I have my wonderful Eastern-/Western-trained medical doctor and a chiropractor who listens to my wacky symptoms and intuitively knows exactly where to work on me in the gentle way that I need. I also have a couple of people who do energy healing work, which I call "hands-on healing," and use related modalities, such as Reiki and craniosacral work. I love a good acupuncture session four times a year for maintenance, and the same for massage.

Of equal importance are my friends who are intuitives, always there when I'm not able to get over the hump of a problem on my own or through other means. They are like therapists except that I don't have to visit a traditional thera-pist's office. (This is a wonderful perk of being in the personal-development industry; I have many amazing and talented friends!) I'm currently mulling over the idea of hiring a nutritionist/ healthy chef to jump-start me to the next level of healthy eating. Over the years, I have tried many health-giving modalities, which provided some wonderful experiences for my spiritual growth and physical healing. Not everything was a good fit, but allowing my intuition to guide me helped narrow down what I wanted. I always learned something from each experience and never felt that I had wasted my time or money.

Step 1: Supplements (Seven Days a Week or As Directed by a Doctor)

If you are going to be medication free in terms of your depression or anxiety, a supplement regime can be very helpful, especially during the initial transition process. It is crucial that you work with a doctor to develop a regime that fits your particular needs. *Do not attempt to do this yourself!* Your doctor can wean you off medication while supplementing you with what your body needs in a more natural form.

The most important person I found was my amazing doctor in Los Angeles, Dr. David Allen. A friend had given him a glowing review, and my gut instinct told me he would be a good fit for me as well. He is a longevity doctor and a genius with blood work, hormones, and figuring out why people just don't feel well. Schooled as a medical doctor, he mostly acts as a naturopathic physician and has chosen that route for his practice. This is where personal preference comes into play, and I'm sure you can find the primary care you need from either an MD or an ND (naturopathic doctor). What I love about the naturopathic approach is that these doctors treat the whole person, taking into account mental, emotional, physical, environmental, and other factors. They recognize that the human body is intelligent and able to heal itself when provided guidance. NDs are real medical doctors; they just don't turn to medication as the first option.

I came to Dr. Allen broken, having just moved to Los Angeles in my early thirties, and stuck on the merry-go-round of antidepressant and anti-anxiety medication. I wanted off. I had gone through ten long years of cycling through different meds and dosages, and I was done. Dr. Allen did a very brief exam, and for the rest of the appointment, I talked to him in his lovely office about how I felt—and he listened. For my entire life, I was used to having my twenty-minute time slot (often reduced to ten minutes) with doctors who did not listen to what I was saying, and simply wrote a prescription and shoved me out the door. Sadly, this is the case for so many.

Dr. Allen ordered extensive blood, urine, and saliva tests, and I went home with a bundle of supplements and a sense of excitement about the start of something wonderful. I had a program to wean myself off of my medication while supplementing with natural versions of what my body lacked. I put my new doctor at the helm of my healing team and always made him aware of what else I was doing. More importantly, I always let my other practitioners in the healing arts know that I was under the care of a primary physician and was on a program of supplements. This is key because most alternative practitioners such as acupuncturists will want to recommend herbs from their own pharmacy. I always declined. I knew that I needed to keep one person (besides myself) in charge of steering the ship, especially regarding any remedies taken orally. By doing so, I was able to stay on course with the supplement program that I had designed with a physician whom I greatly trust.

It is important to note that you may not need to be on these additional supplements for the rest of your life. Each of us is different and unique, and depending on your lifestyle choices and your integration of these pillars, you may eventually be able to wean yourself off of the supplements as well.

If you do any online research, you will come across varying opinions regarding supplements. Some doctors think you should be able to get everything you need from your diet. This may be an option for some people, but if you are rebuilding your body, you need a boost. Rebuilding can take time, and it is important to realize that you didn't get sick overnight, so you can't expect to heal overnight. Slow and steady wins the race.

People ask me all the time what supplements

I take, but I don't feel comfortable sharing my supplement protocol because it will be very different for you and I am not a doctor. In this instance, it is not a "one size fits all" situation. There are many wonderful supplements for the brain and body, and I urge you to buy the best quality you can afford.

Some of the wonderful supplements I have taken over the years (not all at the same time) include melatonin, L-theanine, fish oil, SAM-e, 5-HTP, taurine, DHEA, vitamin D, and a natural thyroid supplement. I have also taken various herbs, and there are some wonderful herbs in tincture form that can help with anxiety in particular. Valerian root and skullcap were both beneficial to me at different times throughout my healing and are easily found over the counter. Bach flower essences can also be a nice addition to your routine, and you don't need to worry about them interacting or interfering with other supplements. They work on a very subtle level but do come preserved in alcohol.

Again, I want to emphasize that these are supplements that worked for my unique situation, and they may not be appropriate for you; I include them just to give you some ideas to explore. It's important to discuss supplements and herbs with your healthcare provider, examining what you are lacking in your system and allowing a trained professional to recommend what you need to take. It is also important to note that during the weaning transition, you may "feel strange," depending on what you are taking. Some strange feelings I had in my body were feelings similar to the first time I took Prozac, and I also experienced a bit of a racing heart and the jitters.

I have a sensitive body, and the journey through supplements really helped me learn new things about my body, such as the need to ease into new substances. Now my doctor knows that if he gives one pill a day to somebody else, I only need half a pill. These "side effects" will clear up after your body is used to the change. If you are ever feeling in distress about something you are taking, you should contact your doctor immediately.

Additional Alternative Therapies

I tend to move a lot and if I'm not available to see my chosen primary doctor, I work with him over the phone. But that leaves other specialty services such as dentists and others up for grabs. When I have to see somebody new, it continually amazes me how uncaring our medical field has become. Dated, unattractive, and uncomfortable waiting rooms and exam rooms; rude staff; long waits; and the feeling of being treated like a number.

Why don't doctors and hospitals understand that when we come for an appointment, we don't feel well! Oh how I wish for the days of home visits—I would pay extra for that service! I recall a time when I was feeling particularly unwell and had to lie down on the floor, because there were no benches or recliners. I just couldn't sit in a chair. I was immediately told that I could not lie down! So much for compassion.

Good doctors, hospitals, and clinics are out there; if you don't like the attention you receive or you feel like your doctor is not listening to you, you have the right to go elsewhere. My doctor is an MD, but he has never once written me a prescription, always treating me with herbs and supplements instead. Maybe a naturopath is the way to go for you, but it will be different for everybody. Be sure to choose wisely based on recommendations, credentials, and your gut feeling about the practitioner. If you have any reservations or a funny feeling, choose a different practitioner, even if it takes you a few tries to find the right one. A good fit is vital to your health and the long-term goal of feeling well.

Once I started having friends who were also on the path to consciousness and wellness, it became easier to find the practitioner that I needed. I was always asking, "Do you know a natural dentist? Do you know a good massage therapist?" I knew that once I had a foot in the door in the community, the right doctor would show up. You can also ask for recommendations at alternative bookstores or attend seminars and events where you will find like-minded people. Take the free magazines and newspapers available at natural grocery stores.

Once you have found somebody you are interested in seeing, book a free consultation. This may only get you ten to fifteen minutes of face time, but that is enough for you to get a feel for how this person works. Notice: Is the office busy and hectic or calm? Did you feel rushed? Did the practitioner answer your questions to your satisfaction? Just feel it out, and ask yourself if this is the right place for you. If not, move along and keep trying until you find a good match. You can also ask for guidance when you sit to meditate and visualize, or ask that a practitioner will cross your path. By taking proactive measures in this way, you are once again telling the Universe what you want and that you are ready for help. Remember that you will be rewarded for your efforts, and much can be found during the search.

While doing your footwork to find the help you need, wonderful things will begin to unfold. Allow yourself to freely go down the path that this unfolding process brings, as one thing often leads to the next. It is much like a puzzle, and the proper piece must be put into place before the rest of the puzzle can be completed. Do not be discouraged if, for example, you see an acupuncturist who didn't fit you or if you didn't like that particular kind of therapy. Try not to write off acupuncture because the first person you saw didn't work out. If you do realize that acupuncture isn't right for you, you can cross if off your list and try something different—perhaps massage or reflexology. Eventually you will find the people and therapies that you like and can help you the best, creating your own personal healing team.

Here are some of the healing modalities I have tried over the years:

Psychiatry
Neurology
Cardiology
Naturopathy
Acupuncture
Homeopathy
Cupping (a part of acupuncture)
Massage
Rifing (with a rife machine)
Zero-point energy system
Chiropractic (alternative and traditional)
Native American shaman healing
Peruvian shaman healing
Past-life regression
Chakra-light crystal bed (John of God)

Energy work (many different types of
    hands-on healing)
Crystal work
Belly massage
Sound healing
Retreats
Channeling
Detox footbaths
Reflexology
Flower remedies
Fire ceremony
Water ceremony
Full-moon rituals
Psychic and psychic-medium readings
Craniosacral therapy
Card readings (tarot and other decks)
Astrological / human design readings
Hellinger family constellation work
    (healing family lineage)
Code singing (into the body)
Qigong
Ear candling
Medical-intuitive work
Every type of healing circle you can
    imagine
Muscle testing (kinesiology)

You can see from this list that there are many
modalities, and I'm sure I have forgotten some. I
would say that I received some benefit from each

of these healing sessions, although some were far better than others. Some treatments led me to the next person or modality I was looking for. Most of the time, I was grasping at straws, looking for something outside of myself to fix all of my problems. When you are chronically ill, you will do whatever it takes to feel better.

At the end of the day, it is up to you to take responsibility for your life. Rather than relying on doctors and healers to fix you, there must be a desire within you to get well. This is why so many programs don't work; people just want to "take the pill" so they can be done. The same is true with my program—you can't simply go through the motions and do the work without really *doing the work!* By this I mean, you need to dig deep. It needs to be uncomfortable for a while and then you will get lasting results.

I have always been blessed to have health insurance, saving me from tens of thousands of dollars in medical bills. However, many of the practitioners I like to see do not accept insurance or are not covered by my policy. Chiropractic care, massage, acupuncture, and energy healing are not covered by my plan, so I am left with large out-of-pocket expenses for these services. Be sure to check with your insurance company to find out which alternative therapies they cover. More and more insurance companies are including some of these modalities, as holistic wellness becomes more mainstream as an "acceptable" complementary option alongside traditional medicine.

There are ways, however, to benefit from services at little to no cost. Massage and acupuncture schools always need people for their students to practice and hone their skills on. (You can even get a low-cost facial from a cosmetology school.) For services that don't require certification, such as energy work, it is sometimes possible to trade services, such as gardening, babysitting, or bookkeeping with the practitioner. Use your imagination—where there is a will there is a way.

Step 2: Take a Walk
(Five to Seven Days a Week)

Don't pass over this section because you assume there isn't anything new to learn about walking. When I coach private clients, walking is the one thing I always recommend. I like it because it's an action element like journaling and meditation. Mindfully putting on your sneakers and heading out the door is an action, and when you do it each day with intention, it will help set up the shift in behavior you are looking for. Throughout this book, when we've looked at behaviors that need to be shifted, we've also assigned an action. Not only is walking a very big action to take but it will make you feel good and has many health benefits as well.

Walking is available to almost everybody, it doesn't cost anything, and you don't need any special equipment to do it. But walking is highly underrated, probably because it isn't fancy and you don't need to buy a membership; you just need to step out of your front door. I am lucky that I can be in nature when I walk out my front door, which allows for some nature meditation at the same time. I can usually walk out of my house with an issue or a problem and have it all figured out by the time I get home. My head is cleared, I'm excited and renewed, and my energy is flowing once more.

Walking can also be a wonderful meditation if done in a mindful way. If you want to try mindful walking, you need to be able to walk undisturbed. Put on sunglasses, a hat, and maybe some earplugs or headphones (without listening to anything). This will usually discourage others from stopping to chat with you so you can stay in your clear head space. One step after another, concentrate on your breath and the steps you take during your walk.

Walking with a friend or loved one on a regular basis is a great way to make sure you stay on task, and it also allows for some focused one-on-one conversation that may not happen otherwise.

Having a regular walking date also keeps you accountable for developing your walking habit. If you don't like to walk alone or you have a hard time getting yourself out the door, pick a walking buddy for at least five days a week. It can be the same person or five different people.

This is one of the action items that I tend to sabotage. It takes a lot of effort for me to get out the door and walk. I will groan about it or complain that it is too hot or too cold or that I have too much writing to get done that day. You know what happens then? I feel bad for the entire day because I have not followed my program. I didn't move my body, and I let myself down. On days like this, I have to dig deep and remember how great I feel after getting home from my walk. I have to remember how clear my head is and how energized I am to get my work done. This will usually get me out the door, because I know that if I don't go, it can start me on a downward spiral. Honestly, who wants that?

Starting my walking program was really hard for me. My self-esteem was so low that I was embarrassed to get out and walk in my own neighborhood. I had self-defeating thoughts, such as *People will think I'm fat* (I've never been overweight) or *People will laugh at me because I'm walking in a skirt and not wearing the right exercise clothes.* I thought everybody was surely peering out of their windows and judging me—it was a great excuse to keep myself in my house. But I knew if I wanted to heal, I just needed to get myself out the door, even if I only went around the block. You may find your own excuses, but there is a remedy to all of them.

If you are pressed for time, think about how you can squeeze in that walk before or after work. If you take a bus to work, put on your sneakers and walk to the bus stop. Tell yourself, *This is my walking time. I'm making this my action item.* If you drive to work, park farther away than usual, put on your sneakers, and do the same thing.

There are days when bad weather such as snow and ice won't allow for walking. On these days think of an alternative action you can do for the day so you stay in your routine. Where I live in California this issue doesn't usually come up for me, but I recently injured both sides of my body—I had a broken right arm and a sprained left arm. My legs were fine, but I was scared that if I fell on my walk, I wouldn't have a good arm to catch my fall and I could risk aggravating my injuries. I tend to trip over my feet a lot, so this was a very real fear and not an excuse. I decided to buy one of those big blow-up yoga exercise balls, and each day I would bounce and make up exercises with the ball. Before I started, I declared that this was replacing my walking time and would be my action item while I recuperated. The intention and replacing of one action with another were enough to get me through that rough patch.

If you don't want to walk alone, set up a Facebook or Meetup page (see the sources at the end of the book) and start a walking group. Get out each day and walk. This is your action item to help rewire your brain. I don't care how far you walk or how long, whether it's around the block or just to the end of your driveway.

Step 3: Nutrition

What you put into your body has an enormous effect on how you feel. If you want to start feeling better, the time to clean up your diet is now. Start by cutting packaged/processed foods, fast food, sugar, junk food, and sodas from your diet. My body will not allow me to eat these foods anymore, and I do not have the desire to do so anyway. I always had the intuitive impression that fast food and soda were not for me, but sugar was my downfall! I loved sweets, mostly in the form of chocolate, cookies, and cake. I'm fortunate to have never had a weight problem, but as I age, I notice my need to be increasingly particular about what I ingest. It makes complete sense to me that I chose sugar as my go-to food choice—but more about that later.

My eating habits changed when I awoke to

being a conscious human being. The two really do go hand in hand: having the awareness that you are a being of energy allows you to care for your body more, and the desire to take good care of it comes naturally. I grew up in a family with a fairly healthy eating culture—brown rice, no soda or chips. It was a good base, but I felt like the odd kid since my friends ate pasta from a can. Until I started to change my eating habits as an adult, I was in the camp of people who thought eating healthy meant you were a hippie. I didn't want any part of that! The organic grocery stores always seemed to be full of barefoot people wearing tie-dyed clothes in rainbow colors, and I felt intimidated by their appearance. So it made sense that my awakening and my introduction to healthy food stores happened in Los Angeles, where so-called normal-looking people (and movie stars) shopped at organic grocery stores.

I believe that healthy eating, like meditation, is okay to obsess about. Once I was introduced to healthy, whole foods, I never looked back. I educated myself on how food was grown and was shocked to learn how we produce our foods commercially. The more I learned, the more upset I got about the pesticides in our vegetables and fruits that we adults and our children are consuming and digesting. And what about the workers who have to spray the chemicals and harvest the food? What about the health of

Mother Earth and the drainage into our water supply?

In order to change my habit for the better in the kitchen, I really needed to learn to fall in love with cooking. This was hard for me, as I never really enjoyed cooking, but that turned around when I moved to Los Angeles in my mid-thirties and bought a Spanish-style house in the Hollywood Hills with a great kitchen. Light came in from all directions, and it was newly remodeled with marble counters and new cabinets. It also came with a vintage O'Keefe & Merritt stove, which was absolutely charming but didn't fit the new décor. Another downside: it always smelled of gas, which doesn't really inspire a person to spend a lot of extra time in the kitchen.

My cooking life changed when I brought in a new Viking range with six burners, a grill, and two ovens. That new stove started me down the path to self-discovery in the kitchen. I scoured magazines for recipes that piqued my interest and tried them all. I went to the permanent West Hollywood Farmer's Market once a week and discovered a love of shopping for fresh ingredients directly from the farmers.

Any change only requires a spark, and if you are like I was and are not thrilled with cooking, I know you can find that spark. Try some easy changes, such as a deep clean of your kitchen and reorganizing your cabinets. Consider buying a new set of pots and pans or knives. (Or sharpen the knives you already have; it will change your prep time for the good!) Bring in some flowers or a big bowl of lemons, organize your fridge, or grow some herbs at your kitchen window or outside. Maybe keeping chickens would spark your interest. Ask your friends for their favorite recipes, find a cooking blog to follow. Do what you need to in order to find that spark that motivates you to prepare nutritious meals.

Once you are on board with taking a good look at what you eat and where your food comes from, I promise your diet will never shift back to your previous habits. Discovering new, healthier ways to eat and places to shop for food can be an exciting adventure. If you have children, you can get them involved by bringing them to the farmer's market on a weekly basis. Whole Foods has a kids club with free fruits and snacks for children, which is a great way to get your children to shop with you. Some smaller organic markets have similar programs for children but may not advertise them, so it's worth asking about if you aren't sure. Who knows? You may inspire them to start a program if they haven't already!

Whether you have children or not, it is important to be mindful of where your food comes from, where it is grown, and whether it supports your local economy. Many local growers love to share information about their crops and will offer preparation and recipe ideas. If you have a particularly wonderful produce person at the market, they will gladly let you taste a piece of fruit or a vegetable if you ask. I want you to get excited about healthy foods and embark on an adventure into this world, especially if it is new to you.

WHERE TO FIND AFFORDABLE ORGANIC FOOD

• Farmer's markets are wonderful places to get reasonably priced produce. Get to know your local farmers and become friends with them. If you shop at the end of the market day, you may find that your friendly farmer will give you a deal that saves you money and saves them from loading those items back into their trucks.

• Pay attention to sales flyers from your organic market and get on its mailing list. Ask the produce manager if they have any blemished fruit or vegetables you can buy at a discount. A lot of produce goes to waste simply because it doesn't look "perfect."

• Grow your own! Nothing tastes as good as fruit or vegetables grown in your own garden.

It is also a wonderful way to spend time with children of all ages; you can get them involved from the seed to the harvest. Not only are you creating enjoyable memories together, but you are giving them a solid platform from which to nurture their own ideas of healthy eating. Even if you don't have room for a garden, you can always grow food in a pot. For example, string beans grow upward and like to climb a post or sticks put in the pot, leaving room at the bottom for other fruits or vegetables.

• Look for a community garden in your area, and let your garden friends and neighbors know that you would love to receive some of their bounty.

SUGAR

I believe most people know that sugar isn't the best substance to consume. Most parents dread the crazy sugar high in their kids after a birthday party, and worry about the potential of cavities caused by juice or gummies. Sugar is in *so* many foods! If you take the time to read food ingredient labels, you will be shocked at the amount of sugar found in everyday items.

Why did I become so down on sugar? Because sugar suppresses our feelings. That is why it is a go-to item for those of us who suffer from depression. Consuming sugar is just another means of medicating the body, like throwing a blanket over our feelings to keep them suppressed. It is easily accessible in the store, costs very little, and tastes good. Because I no longer drink alcohol or take drugs, my body cleverly turned to sugar as a substitute to get the stimulating effects I wanted, showing up in the form of cravings.

Sugar also weakens and suppresses the immune system; I see this all the time in my own family and circle of friends. Sugar bingeing often leads to coming down with a cold or the flu. I learned this through many years of being on and off the sugar train, and many years of tracking and journaling the effects of sugar on my body. There really is nothing good about it.

My hand was always in the cookie jar from an early age, and holidays were a welcome sugar-bliss high. I was always sick as a child with ear infections, colds, and the flu, probably because I was always eating sugar as a way to cope with feeling scared and being in survival mode all the time. An immune system cannot develop properly or function under those abusive conditions.

For me, sugar cravings stemmed from a fractured part of myself that wanted me to stay sick and hidden so I didn't have to face or live life. I wrote about this earlier in the journaling section—about my journey to heal that fractured part of myself that was really just a scared little girl. If you suffer from sugar cravings too, you can explore an answer to this question through writing: Who is shouting at you, "I want cake right now!"? This question alone can fill up an entire journal, so you may want to dedicate a journal to discovering this part of you that is scared and hidden.

Feel free to modify your journal entry: *Who is shouting to me, "I want* _____ *right now!"? Who wants me to stay hidden? Who wants me to stay small and not live my life?* Access the part of yourself that wants to stay medicated with sugary treats. Who is this part of you, and what does he or she want?

When I realized how much sugar was affecting my mood, it became clear that I needed to eliminate it from my diet. This was difficult. I've quit a lot of things, including smoking, but eliminating sugar was by far the hardest—not only because I saw it every day in the store, in restaurants, and in ads, but because it was a powerful medication for me. I went cold turkey, cutting out my daily cookie or cake. I didn't eliminate all sugar; I still ate fruit and the sugar in common foods, like ketchup. The first three days were the hardest, and I had terrible cravings. I felt the part of me that was scared roar up in retaliation that the beast was no longer being fed. The cravings were horrendous; they controlled and begged me to "please just have a little bite of cookie or a chocolate bar." I didn't want to give in to the cravings, so I took to the outdoors to walk it off. Upon my return, I journaled about what I was feeling. I asked myself the question, *What part of me is demanding I eat this sugar?*

Every time a new craving hit, I repeated the process—I wasn't going to let it win. After three days, I felt the worst was over; the cravings had diminished to the point that I felt like a normal functioning human. I was back in the driver's seat, and my body chemistry no longer ruled the roost.

If eliminating sugar from your diet is something you would like to try, I would advise you to shop ahead of time for healthy options to eat. Stock your kitchen with alternative choices, which will help curb your cravings when they hit. For me, raw nuts (which I roasted myself) helped a lot. A cup of tea with a little milk and a handful of nuts made a nice snack around 3:00 PM, when I would normally be searching for a cookie. I also advise you to have your family on board with you for support. Tell them ahead of time what you are doing and that it is fine if they don't want to participate, but ask that they please respect your decision and not offer you sugar.

At first it was important for me to completely break the daily habit of having a piece of cake or a cookie. Eventually I added back in alternative treats from a raw food restaurant or market, which had no effect on my body chemistry. There are some wonderful raw chocolate treats on the market, now found mostly in the fresh-food section of natural grocery stores. Stevia is an herb that is a natural sweeter—and actually much sweeter than refined processed sugar.

I will promise you this: once you get used to alternative natural sweeteners, you will not enjoy treats made with regular sugar. I see more natural and healthy options at health-food markets, such as raw-nut-and-chocolate balls sweetened with dates and coconut, which are a wonderful treat. We make our own at home to save money, and it has become a weekly project to stock up on our homemade raw treats. Since these treats don't give me a high, they don't give me a crash. It is also amazing how just a small amount of these wonderfully healthy treats can be so filling, whereas with sugary treats, I always needed much more.

Start to think about eliminating obvious sugar from your diet and see how you feel about that idea emotionally. Look at your calendar and pick a day when you want to start, preferably a week that isn't stressful. Shop ahead of time to have healthy snacks or natural sweet treats in place. There are also lots of recipes and resources online, as more and more people are learning about the detrimental effects of processed sugar in their diets.

If you need some additional reasons to cut down or eliminate sugar from your diet, here are some proven benefits:

Healthier heart and blood pressure
Lower cholesterol
Healthier skin
Lower risk of diabetes
More balanced mood (less anxiety and irritability, and fewer mood swings)
More awake and alert during the day
Better sleep at night

With all of this said, sometimes you just want to enjoy that birthday cake or holiday cookie. I do indulge in sugar once in a while because I have cleared it out of my body, and it no longer takes hold like an addictive substance. I don't deprive myself of enjoying a treat if it is something I'm interested in. I never eat Halloween candy or anything like that, but if there is handmade chocolate at a social function, I allow myself to have it.

I want to mention to my female readers that we have all experienced that chocolate craving during our cycles and hormone changes. Even when my hormones were perfectly balanced, I still wanted some chocolate during these times. Once I eliminated all the bad sugary treats from my diet, I felt fine having a piece of quality chocolate or one of the raw chocolate treats that I have come to enjoy. A balanced body can help you to make balanced decisions.

Step 4: Sleep

It is considered almost heroic to be one of the lucky few who can survive on four to six hours of sleep per night. I hear people brag about working until the wee hours of the morning and then waking up with the sun to start another day. Upon further investigation, however, it isn't only lack of sleep that is dysfunctional in their lives; there are copious amounts of coffee, stressful job conditions, after-dinner cocktails, and late work nights—a vicious lifestyle cycle that will eventually have harmful effects on a person's mind and body. Sleep is not a luxury; it is a necessity for attaining and sustaining a healthy mind and body.

Most people need about eight hours of uninterrupted sleep in order to function at a healthy capacity. Everywhere I look, there are sleepy people: workers, drivers, schoolchildren. It is impossible to ask so much from our bodies without adequate rest. Lack of sleep sets up a chain reaction that can take a long time to recover from. Impaired motor skills, irritability, reduced immunity, and fatigue are all effects of not getting enough sleep. And sleeping late on the weekends doesn't exactly count, as it really doesn't make up the deficit.

Taking a good look at your lifestyle and where you can make adjustments to get to bed earlier will vastly affect how you do with your work here. Going to bed with sugary sweets or alcohol in your system will delay and interrupt sleep. Staying up too late watching TV or working on your computer doesn't give your brain adequate time to power down before sleep. I learned the hard way about how important sleep can be and now make it a priority in my life to get my nine hours.

Because I know I need more sleep than the average person (nine hours versus eight), I schedule my nights to get to bed at the hour I need in order to get enough sleeping time. I never budge—that is how important it is to me. I learned early on in my illness that if I didn't get enough sleep, my immune system would tank; I became very susceptible to getting sick. Likewise, if I feel like I'm catching something during the day, I know I can beat it if I get my nine hours, and I usually wake up with my symptoms gone.

If you have ever put a young child to bed, you know there has to be a bedtime routine, and sometimes that routine can take an hour: quiet time, bath time, brushing teeth, reading stories, pajamas to wiggle into. But when it comes to our own adult bedtime, we don't give it any attention at all. Try some gentle stretching or easy yoga before bed, or read a book until you feel tired. Keep your phone and computer out of the bedroom so your eyes can adjust to the natural darkness. Clean your bedroom of clutter so it becomes a restful place for you to retire at the end of the day. Then tell everybody proudly that you get eight hours of sleep per night!

My own bedtime routine starts early in the evening by giving the house a straightening so I will find it in good shape when I wake up. This includes my bedroom: if I haven't made my bed that day, I straighten the covers and put clothes in the laundry basket. These may seem like small, uninteresting details, but because they are part of my routine, my brain makes the connection that sleep is coming soon. Like the time I take before meditation to pick up the area first and tidy up, it sends a message. While I'm washing my face and brushing my teeth, I try to let the day drain away with the water, further preparing my brain for sleep. At this point, if I'm not obviously sleepy, I do some stretches before retiring. There are no cell phones allowed in my bedroom either. (I even have one friend who won't have a house phone or a digital clock in her bedroom, preferring to keep both outside, in the hall.)

Some final notes on sleep: Your bed should be

inviting so you want to get into it. Always choose the best sheets you can afford: cotton with a high thread count. In the winter, try flannel sheets or add a featherbed under your mattress cover. Wash your linens weekly so they are fresh, and give your comforter a fluff outside or a spin in the dryer (with no heat). Next, make sure your bedroom is free of clutter, though I realize clutter means different things to all of us. Stacks of magazines, mail, unfolded laundry, exercise equipment—all of these things contribute to clutter. Also keep your bedroom free of dust, and add an air purifier if you suffer from allergies. Finally, if you still can't get to sleep, try sipping chamomile tea right after dinner.

Optional Steps

BLESS YOUR FOOD

Take a moment to stop and be present with your food, acknowledging where it came from and how grateful you are to receive it. This has nothing to do with religion and everything to do with intention. It is truly a sweet gesture, and you can do it when you're alone or with your family and friends. There is no need to be long and drawn out about it; short and simple is fine. If you feel embarrassed by doing this aloud, you can do it silently.

I always bless my food before I eat it but in a quick, informal way. While I'm cooking food for my family, I thank the food I am preparing for nourishing us. I send love to my food while I'm chopping and stirring, knowing that this good energy will enter our bodies. Just a quick "bless you," said with loving intention directed at your food, can help immensely.

I once sat down to eat at a local restaurant, and heard yelling and fighting in the kitchen. I looked at my husband and said, "Let's go. I don't want to eat angry food," and we left. It is important to be a warrior and stand up for your body in any way you can.

If you are familiar with the late Dr. Masaru Emoto's work, you know that water reacts to words that humans speak. It is wonderful that there is now scientific proof of this phenomenon so we aren't labeled as "woo-woo" or crazy. If water is affected by our words, then surely our food and our own bodies are also affected by our words. Always be careful with your words, and choose loving words when blessing your food. Eat love, not hate!

TAKE CLEANSING BATHS

Water is sacred. Entire books have been written about sacred bathing, and the power and energy that water transmits. Water plays a very important part in my life. I grew up in Seattle with a view of the water—I saw it every day. Now that I live in California, I can drive to the ocean in about five minutes, which is bliss for me. For a while, I didn't live near water, so we installed a salt-water swimming pool and designed it to look like a water feature. Even when it was too cold to swim, it was still nice to gaze upon.

Some of my greatest writing moments have come when I have been in the bathtub; that's why I always keep a journal next to it. There are shower people and bath people, and I am of the latter, much preferring a soak in a tub of perfectly warm water with a concoction of my favorite essential oils and salts. If I ever feel like I am getting sick with the flu or a cold, I turn to the bathtub immediately, filling it with remedies and the hottest water I can tolerate, giving the virus little chance to take hold.

There is another way bathing can assist in healing us besides chasing away common illness: it cleanses the auric field. The aura, or electric field, is like an energetic blanket surrounding the body. (If you doubt that you have an aura, you should know that the colors of the aura can be detected by a method called Kirlian photography.) It is the aura that first meets with energies from the outside, and it is often where healers can first spot illness or emotional trauma. Auras also get bogged down with the energy we pick up in daily life, especially if we have been out in a crowd or have deep emotional healing work to do.

A simple cleanse I like to do to help clear and balance my electrical field is a bath filled with Epsom salt, sea salt, and apple cider vinegar (the recipe follows). For the sea salt, you don't need to use an expensive variety infused with oils; in fact, I suggest you use plain sea salt. I like to get my sea salt from the bulk bin at the health-food store. But if you don't want to smell too much like a salad, feel free to add some essential oils.

It is important to get your entire body wet, including your head and hair, and while you are soaking for twenty minutes, keep at least your body in the bath while your head remains above water. I like to take this bath at night, not rinsing afterward and showering the next morning. Two pounds of salt may seem like a lot, but Mother Nature knows what she is doing. There is a reason the ocean is so cleansing—all that salt!

Energy-Field Cleansing Bath

1 pound Epsom Salt
1 pound sea salt
1 cup apple cider vinegar
Optional: lavender essential oil or other scent

Add the ingredients to a tub of warm water and soak for twenty minutes or more. (I know people who like to take this bath before they go on retreat so they have a really clean energy field. It is also a great bath if you have been around too much outside energy, such as a crowded festival.)

A variety of bath soaks are also available on the market. If you don't mind getting your bathtub really dirty, a mud bath can be very detoxifying. This is not like a mud bath at a spa where you slip into gooey mud; at-home mud baths involve putting a small amount of mud into your bath, which doesn't change the consistency of the water too much. Whichever bath you choose, be sure to use it in conjunction with this entire pro-gram and not instead of your program. Needless to say, I am a big fan of baths. I often think (or wish) there isn't anything a bath and a good cup of tea can't fix.

MOVE

Our bodies want to move—they were designed to be in motion. Movement shifts stagnant energy in your system while connecting you to your own body.

I don't like to exercise—I never have. In the 1980s, I tried aerobics but never went to more than a couple of classes. I'm not a gym person, and I don't like exercise equipment. What I love is what I call "random exercise": I take the stairs rather than an elevator or an escalator. I take long walks in my neighborhood or I hike on a nearby trail, enjoying a magnificent view of my small town. When I find myself in a parking lot, I park my car in a spot far away from my destination. I enjoy dancing and grew up dancing ballet, tap, and jazz. I even danced on a kickline much like the one in the Broadway play *A Chorus Line*. After I stopped dancing, I tried yoga, which is amazing for so many reasons.

These days, I swim five days a week and I love it, because it gets me into water, which is always healing for me, and it's a great workout without feeling like exercise. I'm not even a good swimmer! I skip the cap and goggles and just get in, making up my own strokes and swimming until I'm out of breath and feel that I'm done.

Find out what is a good fit for you and is exciting enough for you to do each day. Put on some fun music and dance around your living room like nobody is watching. Dance while you clean your house or with your family. It doesn't have to be for a long time—just enough to get your body moving.

As we age, we want our bodies to feel buoyant.

If you can get yourself into a habit of moving your body each day now, you will be so thankful when you advance to your golden years. Movement is good for *all* parts of the body and directly affects your mental health.

THANK YOUR BODY

We are hard on our bodies in so many ways, but they continue to perform for us day after day. Our bodies monitor and process everything: what we feed them, the function of all our organs, all of our thoughts and feelings, and all of our movement and exercise. But our bodies have become the silent partner in a long-distance relationship. Isn't it time to create a deeper relationship with them?

Our daily thoughts can be somewhat harsh, telling us we are not good enough, not attractive enough, not smart enough, and not thin enough. We get mad at our bodies for failing us physically when we become ill or get injured, and we wonder what they have done when we have a mysterious pain.

I had an epiphany one day that my body was "listening" to me, hearing and taking in every negative word I said, storing away this abuse over the years. Panic set in when I thought about the increased chance that I would develop cancer because of my negativity toward myself. In Chinese medicine, our organs are associated with a feeling or an emotion. For instance, our lungs govern grief, our kidneys govern fear, and our liver holds on to anger. I was filled with anger and grief, and the thought of all of that sitting in my body gave me a clear desire to get to work and free myself from as much old pain as possible.

When I consciously realized that I was emotionally crushing myself, I fell to my knees in sorrow for the emotional abuse I had subjected myself to for decades. It was in that very moment that I made the powerful decision to appreciate my body for all it did by simply saying "thank you": Thank you, body, for putting up with and processing the countless cigarettes, drugs, and alcohol when I was in my twenties. Thank you for letting me know in a very unsubtle way that I had to stop doing all of these things! Thank you, body, for being limber enough to practice ballet, tap, and jazz dancing, and staying mostly injury free. Thank you for processing as best you could all of the unhealthy food I used to eat. Thank you for carrying me on countless walks through nature, and thank you for being strong when I was so ill for many years. Thank you for birthing my beautiful son.

The shift you will feel with this practice is intense and immediate—your body has been waiting for your entire life to hear loving words from you. If you aren't quite in the place where you think you can be kind to your body, try something that has no judgment, such as thanking your body for your hearing, sight, and senses of smell and touch. This can be a wonderful gateway to the best relationship you will ever have with your physical self.

ENERGY CHECK

Another helpful thing I do first thing in the morning, while still in bed or in the shower, is to perform an energy check on myself. I do this because I am an empath, and I feel the feelings of others. I already know how the world is doing that day and what the weather is like based on how I feel when I open my eyes. Even if you do and eat the exact same things every day, you will *feel* different each day.

We all have our own biorhythms based on planetary influence, our sleep pattern from the night before, and so on. While I'm performing a quick check of my body's energy, I also check on my internal organs to see if any areas need attention. This task is different for each person, as we all perceive energy differently. Some people are more in tune than others, although I truly believe it is something everybody can learn to do.

Some of us see (clairvoyance), some hear (clairaudience), and some feel (clairsentience). I have a bit of all three, but my main sense is clair-sentience, and my clairvoyance is in my mind's eye. For example, I don't see spirits with my physical eyes; I sense their presence and "see" them in my mind.

My energy check looks something like this: I imagine a light beam slowly scanning my entire body (much like that of a photocopier copying with its lid open). I begin at my toes and scan my body with the light beam. Taking my time, I witness my body's energy and pay attention to anything that might catch my "seeing" eye. Slowly I work up my entire body and continue the light beam to about a foot over my head. Wonky energy might show up as a dark spot, a cloudy area, or a mushy-looking glob. Or my "feeling" sensation may indicate a blockage, telling me to stop and deliver light to a particular area.

As I scan the trunk of my body, I listen care-fully with my inner senses for anything my organs have to report. My liver has indicated it would like some attention, and I take note of that to make a decision later on the best course of treatment. In the case of my liver, I tune in to see what it wants: perhaps a cleanse, an oil massage, positive affirmations, or a homeopathic remedy. While doing your energy check, you can also take note of your chakras (energy centers in your body) to see if any of them need clearing.

Your energy check may look completely different from mine, and it may take only a minute or much longer. The important thing to remember is to not judge what comes up. Your session will be perfect for who you are and how you work with your body.

When you first start out, you may not sense anything and may think it is a waste of your time. But you don't know how to play the piano when you first sit down either; it takes practice—and the results are worth the effort. Again, we all function differently, so why not play around with the idea and see how it goes for you. (I want to note that this practice should not replace any advice from your doctor. If you do sense something, consider bringing it to their attention.)

5

Pillar Four:
Find Your Tribe

A lot of formal programs (diet and exercise programs in particular) recommend having a buddy, a friend, or a sponsor. For some programs this is because they want you to be accountable to somebody other than yourself, and for others it can be more of a confessional relationship. For me it is all about community—about having a friend or a group of friends you can call at any time and just be you.

Community means having somebody to talk to when you are having a bad day and when you don't want to work at your program; somebody who won't judge you and will lend a compassionate, listening ear; somebody who leaves you feeling good after a conversation, not drained. Having a good friend isn't about feeling bad and having to confess—or worse, needing to check in and lie about your behaviors. Finding your tribe is about having fellow compassionate human beings who have your back, whether they have been in your shoes or not.

If you don't have a friend in your life now who can fulfill this purpose, you may find somebody while you go through the process of working at this program. In this section about finding your tribe, I will ask you to step outside of your world a bit by volunteering, having fun, and finding purpose. All of these offer myriad opportunities to meet new and wonderful people who could become part of your tribe.

Remember: when you ask the Universe, it responds in kind. If your heart is yearning for a supportive friendship, ask at the beginning or end of your meditation or in your journaling work to be sent a new friend who can be supportive of you. And perhaps you can be supportive of him or her too.

I mentioned volunteer work, and this will become important for you while you are giving back to your community. This is different from our work earlier of asking the Universe, "How may I be of service today?" Volunteer work is regular, whereas the former is more spontaneous, and you are acting almost like a human angel. I will also ask you to get out and have fun, and although it may sound strange to tell people to have fun, you would be surprised by how many people do not have fun—or don't even know how.

Step 1: Call a Friend
(Once a Week, Minimum)

A very important step in the process is to have a friend you can reach out to who will lend a listening and nonjudgmental ear. We all want to be heard; it is human nature at its most basic level to want to be validated and witnessed by another. This is why social media is so popular, allowing people to post their status for all to witness. When we do this, we get a sense of satisfaction that we have somehow been heard. We then spend the next few hours checking to see who "heard" us, and when few people respond or a reply isn't to our liking, we begin a spiraling descent into feelings of low self-worth. There is an entire generation now that knows nothing but this new way of social interaction.

It is important in my program to reach out and call a friend, especially if you are feeling blue, bored, or "out of it." Connecting with a friend in a very real way is good tonic for your soul. Think back to how good you felt the last time you ended a phone call with a trusted friend. If you are prone to depression, it is imperative that you have your tribe—your community of friends that you can call upon even if you have nothing to say. Making this connection is vital to your health and well-being, and I urge you to not discount this critical step. This would be a good time for me reiterate that besides calling a friend, if you are using the help of a therapist in any form, please continue to do so.

By the time I had healed enough to get off the sofa, I didn't have many friends left. They had slowly left my reality, as they no longer wanted to put up with my excuses for not going out. If I didn't even know what was wrong with me or how to heal myself, how could I expect them to stick around for so many years? I had nothing to give in a friendship, and there is only so long people will put up with a one-sided relationship. I think if I'd had a disease that people could understand, it may have been different, but I don't fault anybody for leaving me. It also seemed easier to not have any friends, because I was tired of explaining how poorly I felt and tired of hearing, "You just need to get out of the house!"

Now, years on, I am blessed to have a wonderful community of friends. Having a little more experience and wisdom in my middle-age years has been a gift that allows me to enjoy healthy friendships. And face-to-face interaction is vital: a tea date, a walk together—anything in person so that two sets of eyes can gaze upon each other and arms can reach out in a warm embrace, exchanging energy.

You may notice that as you get healthier, you attract different types of people—healthy people attract healthy people. It is also during your healing process that you may feel the need to let go of some friends who no longer resonate with you. This is a natural part of evolving to a higher-level mind, body, and spirit. You don't *have* to let go of anybody, but if such feelings start to percolate in you, it is time to decide whether certain people should still be in your circle of friends. This can be tricky because, at one time, the friendship may have been wonderful. As you shift and change, however, not all friendships are meant to last. This can be felt on both sides: From your side, you are shifting into a higher level of consciousness and what fed your relationship before may no longer feed it, dragging you down. From your friend's perspective, you have changed, and they may find that threatening. Some friendships can absolutely withstand these changes, and you can ebb and flow together in your growth—the ultimate goal. But it is equally okay to let each other go. It is up to you whether you need to have a conversation about this or not; sometimes friends just drift apart.

Often, when we are in an unhealthy state, we have like-minded friends who feed on our perceived weaknesses. This is human nature. It is not malicious; it is just being human. I mention this only so that you are prepared to allow a friend to drift away and don't spend a lot of time with feelings of guilt. If you are familiar with the law of attraction, it applies to friendships as well. Like attracts like, so it would make sense that you may have some changes in your friendships as you change your life.

In my years of life experience, I have noticed that, in general, people tend to fall into one of two categories when it comes to friends: they either clam up and isolate themselves, never reaching out for help, or, at the other extreme, they are not able to make a single decision without discussing it with a friend. Ideally, we strive for balance in our lives, allowing the pendulum to swing in the middle rather than wildly to one side or the other.

If you fall into the camp of never wanting to be alone or always needing to be busy, there is some work for you to do! Take time to write about why you don't like being alone. What is your fear and where is it coming from? If you are always keeping yourself busy, ask yourself, *What would happen if I had an entirely clear day, with nothing on my schedule? How does that make me feel?* People who keep busy on purpose are often emotionally wounded, not wanting to be left with their feelings.

If you retreat, hide away, and isolate, it is vital to reach out of your cave to connect with others.

WHY DO WE ISOLATE?

When we isolate from others, we are engaging in yet another form of self-sabotage. But when we can simply identify on paper the patterns we have created, we can easily shift them—they don't seem as monumental. I spent many, many years isolating myself from friends. Below are some of the excuses I made to not pick up the phone. Maybe you will recognize some of your own or similar patterns in yourself.

I don't want to burden others with my problems.

I'm so depressed, and I don't have anything interesting to say.

I'm afraid my friends will judge me.

I don't feel I have any real friends left because I have spent so much time isolating myself.

I feel I have outgrown my friends and they wouldn't understand me now.

If I tell my friends how I really feel, they will run the other way and never come back.

If I tell my friends how I really feel, they will think I am strange, weird, or mentally ill.

I don't want to bother anybody; they are probably busy anyway.

It is weak to ask for help; I don't want to appear needy.

It is just safer to keep to myself in my cave.

This is what I'm used to—just me, myself, and I.

Why rock the boat? I'm okay.

Sadly, many of these statements are truth for a lot of us. I want to share this very important idea: When you don't pick up the phone and call a friend, you are denying them the chance to help you. Who are you to judge how they feel or how they will respond to you? It isn't your business to project how your friend will feel. Take a moment to imagine what it would be like if a good friend of yours was in pain but didn't pick up the phone to call you, because they had all of these self-limiting beliefs stuck in their head.

It doesn't feel good, does it? **For every relationship, when two people come together, it is always for the purpose of knowing the self better.** Everyone at all the different times in your life has things to offer you; they have opportunities to present to you and you to them. Relationships are mirrors for us: We often see in another what we must learn for ourselves. It is a brilliant system—in helping yourself, you are also helping your friend. What does it feel like to call a friend now, after this new realization?

A lot of the time, just having a realization can shift and resolve an issue. Patterns and beliefs we have held for a very long time usually need a little help in order to change.

Try this journaling exercise: for every behavior you can list, write down a counteraction to that behavior. Remember: writing with a pen and paper is much more powerful than simply thinking about the task. Writing makes your action more real and allows you to go deeper than you would normally go with just your thoughts.

As an example, here are my counterstatements to the excuses I listed on page 173:

I don't want to burden others with my problems.
Friendships are not a burden; they are give and take, share and receive.

I'm so depressed, and I don't have anything interesting to say.
It is okay to just be silent on the phone.

I'm afraid my friends will judge me.
Turn the tables; would I judge my friend?

I don't feel I have any real friends left because I have spent so much time isolating myself.
This is something I can work on by going out and connecting with new people. But if I think hard, I bet there is a childhood friend who really knows me, and I can still connect with them.

I feel I have outgrown my friends and they wouldn't understand me now.
I know it is natural to sometimes grow apart from friends when our interests and lives change.

If I tell my friends how I really feel, they will run the other way and never come back.
Again, would I do that to somebody? No. If they do run away, they are probably just feeling scared too.

If I tell my friends how I really feel, they will think I am strange, weird, or mentally ill.
Ha! So what. Who wants to be "normal"?

I don't want to bother anybody; they are probably busy anyway.
Classic self-sabotage. I can pick up the phone and call. If they are busy, I can leave a message and they will call when they are available.

It is weak to ask for help; I don't want to appear needy.
Asking for help is actually a sign of strength. Own it and honor your courage.

It is just safer to keep to myself in my cave.
Safe does feel good—the world can be scary. But I feel ready to peep out. Making the call is a great first step.

This is what I'm used to—just me, myself, and I.
Yes, but the status quo is no longer working, and I need to make a change.

Why rock the boat? I'm okay.
Yes, I am okay, but I am not thriving, and I want to live fully!

You know that feeling when you worry and obsess about something you plan to do, and then the time comes to do it and it turns out it wasn't a big deal? Like when you had to act in the elementary school play and you were afraid, but when you were done, you were so happy? That is the feeling you will get after you reach out and call a friend for help. When you end the call, you will feel elevated not only because you made a heart connection with a friend but because you have begun to shift a behavioral pattern.

If you are a cave dweller, set up a goal for yourself. Perhaps start with one call a week and see how that feels. (Texting does not count!) If you don't end up making the call that week, write down the reasons why, without editing your thoughts. After you get through all the usual excuses of being busy or sick, look for the real reason, and rather than judging yourself, come up with a plan that can get you closer to making that call.

Making the phone call is another physical action that will help shift a pattern, and it brings you into a heart connection with another person. Besides making the phone call to a friend, it is just as important to get out and socialize in general. If you work at home or are a stay-at-home parent, you can get into your daily routine and be too worn out to leave the house. Leave the house anyway, for social reasons. The easiest way is to go for a walking or hiking date, a coffee or tea break, a leisurely lunch, or a shopping date. We are not meant to be alone, and we aren't meant to do our soul work alone—we need each other.

The bigger the houses we build, the more social-media structure we create and the more we isolate. No longer are there three generations under one roof; many of us do not have any family around at all. Usually the last thing people want to do when they are going through changes is to socialize, but it is then that they need it the most. Create the village you need if it doesn't exist, and I promise you that the other people who are craving and needing the same thing you are will find you.

If you are not attending events or aren't creating them yourself, ask yourself what the reasons are and write about them. Once they are on paper, you will easily see that your excuses don't warrant your staying home or deciding not to invite people over. Here are some common excuses:

I have nothing to wear.
My house is messy; I don't like my
  house.
I don't have / can't afford a babysitter.
I have to get up early in the morning.
I'm shy and hate meeting new people.
I don't cook; I have nothing to bring.
I'm not good at games, conversation,
  or meeting new people.
I just don't know how to be a host/
  hostess.
Nobody will come; everybody will
  cancel.
I don't like the way I look today.

When you see your excuses written down, they are very real but also very fixable. I invite you to spend less time thinking of ways to stay home and more time on the wonderful feeling you have after you have had a great time socializing. I fully show up with who I am now, perceived flaws and all. If it is a potluck, I tell the hostess I'm too busy with my child and my business and ask if I can bring something made from the deli or help in a different way. If I entertain at my own home, I ask one friend to show up early to be by my side and help with last-minute things to do.

That way, one guest is already there, and I get to bypass the awkwardness of waiting for people to show up. There is always a way to get through any scenario in life; sometimes we have to get creative. But most of the time, we only need to make the effort to come up with a solution. There is *always* a solution.

Step 2: Perform Service Work or Give Back

Service work must be done in the energy of giving, not receiving. You must not expect anything in return or go into it for the purpose of helping yourself feel better. Selfless service work carries and creates a very high vibration; in doing the work, you naturally help yourself too. But try not to enter into doing service work for this reason alone.

Many people volunteer their time to help others because they feel they can make a difference in somebody's life. But they may also have an agenda they are not aware of. I find this happens most often when people work with small children and animals. With people, what happens is that a dynamic is created where the volunteer is actually trying to save the other person "in need," and if they can just get this person to choose differently they will ultimately correct what went wrong in their own life. The truth of the matter is that this kind of volunteer is putting his or her own beliefs onto the other. It is all about the energy.

A good way to get into service work is to sit in meditation with this topic for a period of time and ask the Spirit to assist in finding a good match for you. Come to it with an open, pure heart and then watch for what is presented to you. When service work is approached in this way, it will create a more balanced energy between you and those who you serve.

I am an equestrian; I love horses, as they are very grounding and truth-telling creatures. At one point I was riding a school horse several times per week that I had fallen in love with immediately. She was in what is called a "rental string," a group of horses taken on trail rides, and she was the underdog at the barn. Because she was low in the pecking order, the other horses wouldn't let her eat, and she was underweight. My riding instructor brought her extra food to try to bulk her up, and one day he told me she was available for purchase.

I wanted to have her as my very own, and somehow the money for the purchase came to me easily and suddenly. It was the exact amount I needed, and I took this as a sign. Even though the barn was asking way too much for the horse, there was no stopping me. I had her checked by a vet, who said she would need a lot of medical care, antibiotics, special food to gain weight, and chiropractic care. This still didn't stop me—by now I was a woman on a mission, and I would buy that horse and heal her no matter what it took! I named her Angel, and we moved her into a barn with her own stall. It was very large (to accommodate her size), warm, and dry, with her own food and water.

What happened next shocked me and sent me into a tailspin. She *hated* the stall. She kicked at the door and whinnied loudly. Within minutes, I heard from other people that they would never buy a horse from a rental string for many reasons—one of them being that these horses are used to living in a herd. Why hadn't anybody told me this before? And if they had, would I have listened? Probably not. I left her there overnight. Driving home I thought, *What in the world have I just done? I've made a huge mistake.*

I continued to get Angel in good physical condition with medicine and various healing techniques, and it worked. Her physical body was healing, but her mental state was bad. Very early each morning, I went to the barn to feed and groom her and have a quiet walk with her in the ring. We bonded fast and I adored her.

One day during a lesson, she bucked me off, twice. This had never happened before, as she had always been a gentle giant. My instructor gave it a try, and she bucked him off too. Something was wrong, and soon, I was spending money each day to have a trainer come to work with her. The costs mounted, leaving me with huge bills and a broken spirit. It became very clear to me that I needed to find her a new home that could accommodate her needs. Giving her back to the original barn was not an option, however, as she would become thin and sick again.

I found a home for her out in the country with other barn animals and a little girl. It was perfect. On the last day before she was to be loaded up and moved, we went for our morning walk, and as I was walking her back to her stall, I noticed a chunk of her tail had come loose and was trailing behind her. I stopped and grabbed the tail hair and put it in my pocket. I knew in my heart this was a gift from my Angel.

To say it was sad to see her go would be an understatement. I cried for weeks, grieving her loss, but felt solace knowing that she was where she belonged. I heard through the grapevine that she was happy, and I had to be satisfied with that. When it was all said and done, I was left with what felt like a giant pile of mashed potatoes on my plate. I sat in meditation, wondering what in the world all of that was about, and I blamed myself for making a poor decision and being unable to power through it.

As I peeled back the layers of feelings and emotions, I realized that I had projected my own feelings of lack onto the horse. In doing what I thought was a good thing (saving my horse), *what I was really doing was trying to save a part of myself that needed saving—one that I wasn't willing to look at.* Projection is a defense mechanism; when you project onto another, there is a part of you that knows there cannot be a resolution because you cannot change that other person or animal. In my case, as long as I projected my need to be saved onto the horse, I wouldn't have to look at my own life. I acted from a place of fear that the horse did not choose the life it was supposed to choose, but in reality, my motivation was selfish. To this day I have Angel's tail bits wrapped with a ribbon on my altar. It is a beautiful reminder of the lesson I went through with her, and I will always be grateful.

Your volunteer work should not be something you rush into. A really good way to find out what is a good fit for you is to make a list of what types of work might interest you. Think about broad categories first, such as working with children, animals, the environment, the elderly, or the homeless. Next, write about the way in which you would like to work: Do you want to work alone or with others? Do you want to be seen or hidden away in an office? Would you prefer clerical work or more hands-on work with the people or animals?

There is absolutely a lid for every pot when it

comes to service work. There are organizations online (see "Additional Resources" on page 203) that list volunteer opportunities by city; this can be a great jumping-off point. My mother is in her mideighties and does service work at a retirement home where she would eventually like to live. She does many tasks, from filing to helping with parties for the residents, and it has the side effect of making her feel comfortable in a future home. Also, remember that service work doesn't always have to be done through an organization; maybe you can adopt a neighbor who is elderly or disabled. Whatever you choose, the idea is to give back selflessly.

Step 3: Have a Purpose

I always find it interesting that when I meet an elderly person who is happy and vibrant and in good health, they seem to have a purpose for living, or as the French say, a *raison d'être*. For some it may be a hobby, or perhaps they help fellow community members in need (tutoring young children, or maybe feeding the birds every morning). It doesn't matter what it is as long as there is something for them to look forward to each day that makes them feel useful.

It is interesting to note that feeling bored with life is a symptom of depression. You don't want to enjoy life, so you complain that you are bored. See how sneaky and tricky we are? People who are depressed don't feel they have a purpose; they aren't on track with life.

It really doesn't matter what your purpose is; it will be different for everybody, and it will probably change several times throughout your life. Scores of books have been written to help people find their purpose, but all you need is to take some time to explore.

As we age, our purpose changes, as the life of a student is very much different from that of a parent or a retired person. A college student is concentrating on studying, doing well in school, and graduating; a parent is trying to get through each day without falling apart; and an elderly person is trying to stay healthy and keep busy. Within each of these contexts, you need to have something more—a reason to get up in the morning besides school, work, or children.

I believe we have all come to earth to learn to give and receive love, and beyond that, it comes down to personal preference. If you don't know what your purpose is beyond your daily life, take some time with your journal to explore:

- What do you look forward to when you first wake up in the morning?
- What really excites you?

- We have all heard the phrase, "Whatever floats your boat." Write down some ideas about this and don't edit yourself; go ahead and be crazy with it.

My purpose is to help as many people as possible to awaken to their greatest potential. This is what excites and motivates me, and what I look forward to each day. But there are other things I look forward to, such as my crafting time, making sure the wild birds have a place to bathe and drink, and communing with nature, filling up my soul in a way that only nature can.

Throughout my life, I have witnessed many people who have found their purpose—picking up trash on the beach or feeding and caring for feral cats. I know a man who photographed his neighborhood as the seasons changed and shared the photos with his neighbors. There is usually a "bird lady" in every park, feeding pigeons, seagulls, or ducks. I have seen people start neighborhood gardens on their own property and bask in the joy of watching people come to work there, planting, harvesting, or simply reading in the sanctuary they have created. Another garden in my old neighborhood was made of beautiful mosaics. The owners of both of these gardens found a great sense of purpose offering their space to their community.

Step 4: Have Fun! (Every Day)

Most of us don't know how to have fun anymore. We have grown more serious as we slip further into our daily routine of work and family obligations. Why is it that we feel we don't deserve to have fun? Here are some reasons I came up with during my healing process:

> If I have fun, I am not tending to my depression.
> If I have fun, people will expect more of me because that means I have no problems.
> If I have fun, that means I am happy, and the hurt part inside of me will not allow for that. It wants to continue to be heard.
> If I have fun, more people will notice me, and I don't want to be noticed.
> If I have fun, the other shoe will drop and something bad will happen. I just don't deserve to be happy.
> If I have fun, it will feel uncomfortable for me—I'm not used to it
> If I have fun, people will think I'm okay, and I'm not okay; I'm suffering.

Do any of these statements sound familiar to you? They come from a place of deep wounds that needs to be recognized and healed through your dedication to your healing practice. Reading statements like these can make you feel like it is impossible to feel happy or have fun, but I can assure you—without a doubt—that it is possible, with time and commitment to your well-being.

The easiest way to see what fun looks like is to watch young children at play. Children are totally in the present moment. They don't care who is watching them; they never feel that people are judging them; they don't feel like they aren't good enough. Their spirits soar, as they are fully enveloped in the freedom of who they really are. If the leaders of the world came together to watch little children play and held their world meetings on the playground, there would be no more war. Allow yourself to have fun!

If you are having trouble finding your fun, take some time to imagine yourself laughing, and being happy and silly. What are you doing in this image? Frolicking in the ocean? Dancing? Running through a meadow with abandon? Playing baseball? After you have spent some time imagining, describe in your journal what you experienced. Note some ideas that you think would be fun for you. Remember: This is your crazy list. You don't have to actually do these things, but it is a great exercise to get your fun juices flowing.

Spend more time in a happier state of mind than in a depressive one. Once you have your list of fun things to do, recognize how it makes you feel. Are you feeling excited about trying some of your ideas or are you scared? Did feelings of unworthiness come up for you? Write about all of your feelings around these thoughts, then try to write down some counteractions to these thoughts. If you haven't guessed by now, yes, these are action steps to help shift you out of the way you presently think. We want to shift you into happiness!

I'm still working on having fun. It isn't as hard for me as it used to be, but I notice that I sometimes slip back into my old ways of thinking. Fortunately, I catch myself right away: I notice the thought, pause and take a breath, and then send the thought away.

Some ways that I like to have fun are:

Riding horses

Going out into nature with my son and exploring without a plan

Dancing in my living room

Having an unexpected picnic

Berry picking or hiking in the woods and recalling the utter silliness and abandon that children do so well

Calling a friend who always gives me the biggest belly laugh

Acting out of character and surprising my
family with spontaneity

Again, it doesn't matter what your idea of
fun is; what is fun for you may not be fun for
somebody else. (I don't think skydiving would be
fun for me!) Find your fun—you deserve it, and
yes, you are worth it. When you can learn and
allow yourself to find the lightness and silliness
in everyday things, you will be rewarded with a
lifetime of fun-filled memories.

I want to end my Unmedicated Program on
an uplifting note so you finish this book feeling
happy and upbeat. Remember to have a big belly
laugh, let down your guard, and enjoy life more.
I promise you that as you heal yourself, it will be
much easier to allow yourself to have fun. It will
simply become a normal part of who you are.

Unmedicated Program Review

Remember what I wrote about earlier in the book: **you need to set up a series of actions so that a shift may occur**. Remember that it is in the *doing* that the shift can happen. Take action—receive the shift. Your goal is to live your life healthy and whole, whether that means becoming unmedicated from antidepressant and anti-anxiety medications, or any other ways you may self-medicate, or creating a new foundation—a new way of being—dedicated to healing and improving your quality of life.

By working at this program, you are taking actions contrary to the inner voice that tells you things like *I am not good enough*. The key to working any program successfully is to organize your life so you have every possible chance to get it done. Don't be hard on yourself if it takes you time to get into a routine. With that said, don't let yourself get away with too many excuses either, because there are big feelings hiding under there that need your loving attention!

The Four Pillars to Shifting Your Life

Pillar One: Clear Your Mind
- Meditate in silence for ten to thirty minutes each day.
- Connect with nature.

Pillar Two: Nurture Your Spirit
- Journal with purpose; get what is in your head out on paper; reach deeper levels.
- Write a letter to the wounded part of yourself.
- Be creative!
- Ask, "How may I be of service today?"

Pillar Three: Strengthen Your Body
- Walk five days a week or more.
- Build your body and brain with supplements and healthy foods.

Pillar Four: Find Your Tribe
- Call a friend.
- Do service work and give back.
- Find your purpose.
- Have fun!

My Typical Day in Action

Maybe you are curious about what a typical day looks like for me. I'm happy to share the details with you so you can have a clearer picture of what the Unmedicated Program looks like in action. Remember: it may seem like there is a lot here, but it really does flow seamlessly through my day after many years of practice.

- I wake up and immediately notice the day— what the weather is and how I feel. I take note of how I slept. Before I had my son, I did my energy check before I got up, but these days, I need to get right up and get his day started, so I save the energy check for the shower or do it after he has left for school.

- When I have the house to myself, I head straight into my studio and light a candle and incense for my meditation session. If I can't settle down after taking some deep breaths, I'll use some assistance from a guided meditation or meditation music. I do ten to thirty minutes of meditation.

- After meditation, I move into ten to twenty minutes of journaling. I have a few different journals going: one is dedicated to writing about my son, one is dedicated to my ongoing emotional healing, and one is dedicated to work. I don't write in all three each day—that would be too much!

- After I journal, I take my morning walk outside my front door, getting in about twenty minutes of walk time.

- At this point, it is time for my DailyOM writing and editing work, and because I work at home (I need the silence), I have the luxury of rearranging my schedule to accommodate my needs. I am thankful every day for this blessing.

- All of my meals and snacks are healthy, and this is carried over to the office, where my employees are offered an organic macrobiotic meal for lunch each day.

- I do service work twice a week, and if the weather is cooperating, I get out into my garden every day, even if I just say hello. In warmer weather, I'm outside as much as possible with my laptop.

- If I don't have time for my creativity practice during the day, I sometimes fit it into my evening by sitting with a weaving project, coloring with my family, or knitting.

- I call a friend about once a week now, or more when I need it, and my friends usually end up calling me just in the moment when I think I may need them. (Funny how that happens!)

- My fun is sprinkled here and there during the week but mostly shows up on the weekends, when I ride horses with friends.

- You can see that my meditation, journaling, and walking are very much cemented in my everyday schedule—those are just not optional at all. The other items are less rigid now that I am stable and I don't need to do them as often, but they still get done.

- If I ever find myself feeling like I don't want to do these things, I take time to feel into my hesitation to see if I'm self-sabotaging or maybe getting sick. At this place in my healing, I can allow myself to take a day off and it doesn't affect me, but I make the *conscious* decision to take that day off. My program is like second nature to me now— it's how I live. And it will become that way for you too.

Afterword

When I began writing this book, I had been working my program for about seventeen years. I am still free of antidepressants and anti-anxiety medications, although I take a small dose of an antianxiety medication for plane travel or when I have a lot of dental work done. I have a rewarding life as a cofounder of the DailyOM website and as an author, helping millions of people all over the globe with my writing career. It is an honor and a privilege to serve humanity in this way.

As I have advanced into middle age, I have come to realize that I will never fully heal myself in this lifetime. This was shocking to me to grasp. But I have learned that, in fact, this can be a positive in my life, as I will always have one foot in the reality of what it is like to live with emotional pain and trauma. It is necessary for me to always have my experience at the ready so I can serve others. This is a sacrifice I am willing to make.

If I were completely free of all pain and suffering, I'm not sure I would have the motivation to keep up my service work (helping those with emotional pain) the way I do now. This is my path, however, and I have come to a place of peace with it. This does not need to be *your* path, as it is absolutely possible to live a happy and fulfilled life of recovery from depression, anxiety, emotional pain, and trauma. Even though I am well aware of my pain, I am no longer suffering, and I continue to work at my program based on how much I need to do at any given time.

If I feel myself slipping into old patterns, I quickly dive into each of the four pillars 100 percent, until I am stable enough to pull back ever so slightly. I know myself well enough to dance the dance, and I understand where my perfect point of balance resides.

I want to say to all of my readers that if I can do this, so can you. I've gone from a scared, reclusive, sick person to living my life in the driver's seat, greeting each day with possibility. You are a courageous human. I know this because you are reading this book! You want a shift, and I guarantee that it is possible if you do the work. And do you know what is tremendously beautiful? As you do the work, you are not only helping yourself but all of humanity. It is the ultimate hundredth monkey effect: if enough people change, we can create changes in areas of the globe where we have never even visited.

When enough people decide to do the work, it keeps enough energy of love and grace here to supply other people with it when they need it. And when they take it, they begin to flower and change the world too. This is grace in action: by healing yourself, you heal your fellow humans. For me, I came here to change the world by changing myself.

You are a bright and shining star, and I want nothing more than for you to shine as brightly as you want to. I wish you well on your healing journey.

Additional Resources

MadisynTaylor.com
   Madisyn's personal website, with information about *Unmedicated*, additional products, and more.

DailyOM (DailyOM.com)
   Madisyn's company, which includes free inspirational emails delivered to your inbox daily, plus online courses, guided meditations, and Madisyn's other books.

Previous Books
   • *DailyOM: Inspirational Thoughts for a Happy, Healthy, and Fulfilling Day* (Hay House, 2008)
   • *DailyOM: Learning to Live* (Hay House, 2010)

Guided Meditations (CD or download)
Unmedicated Meditation
   • *Meditation for Forgiveness*
   • *Meditation for the Highly Sensitive Person*
   • *Eagle Meditation*

- *Releasing Fire Meditation*
  (See MadisynTaylor.com or DailyOM.com for more updates.)

Online Courses (DailyOM.com)
- Living As a Highly Sensitive Person in an Insensitive World
- Meditation for Beginners
- Learning to Live
- Personal Rituals for Sacred Healing
  (See MadisynTaylor.com or DailyOM .com for more updates.)

Contributing Author
- *No Mistakes: How You Can Change Adversity into Abundance* by Madisyn Taylor, Sunny Dawn Johnston, and HeatherAsh Amara (Hierophant Publishing, 2013)
- *Modern-Day Miracles: Miraculous Moments and Extraordinary Stories from People All Over the World Whose Lives Have Been Touched by Louise L. Hay* by Louise L. Hay and Friends (Hay House, 2010)

Other Resources
- Call 911 if you are in distress.
- Suicide Prevention Hotline: 1-800-273-8255

- SuicidePreventionLifeline.org: Help is available twenty-four hours a day, every day.
- Crisis Text Line: Text "HOME" to 741741 from anywhere in the United States, any time, about any type of crisis.
- National Alliance on Mental Illness: Nami.org
- Meetup.com: This is a great resource for finding like-minded people in your neighborhood to do fun and interesting things with! You can also organize a Meetup group yourself.
- VolunteerMatch.org: This organization provides a list of volunteer opportunities near you.
- See MadisynTaylor.com for additional and updated resources.

About the Author

Madisyn Taylor is the cofounder and editor in chief of DailyOM. She is an award-winning and bestselling author of two previous books, including *DailyOM: Inspirational Thoughts for a Happy, Healthy, and Fulfilling Day* and *DailyOM: Learning to Live*, and her books have been translated into more than fifteen languages. Madisyn has also been a contributing author for Oprah.com and writes online courses and guided meditations for DailyOM. She was previously a regular host on XM Satellite Radio and is a popular guest on many current radio shows. Her *Meditation for the Highly Sensitive Person* was number 1 on the New Age album charts for Billboard, Amazon, and iTunes. She was also featured in the movie *Sensitive—The Untold Story* (2015), a documentary about the highly sensitive trait. Madisyn resides in Santa Barbara, California. In her spare time you can find Madisyn riding horses, meditating by the beach, or in her garden. You can find her work at DailyOM.com or MadisynTaylor.com.

Books are produced in the United States using U.S.-based materials

Books are printed using a revolutionary new process called THINKtech™ that lowers energy usage by 70% and increases overall quality

Books are durable and flexible because of smythe-sewing

Paper is sourced using environmentally responsible foresting methods and the paper is acid-free

Center Point Large Print
600 Brooks Road / PO Box 1
Thorndike, ME 04986-0001 USA

(207) 568-3717

US & Canada:
1 800 929-9108
www.centerpointlargeprint.com